The
Making
of a
Missionary

The
Making
of a
Missionary
Taking the Mystery out of Missions

Jay and Sunny
McLaughlin

Pleasant Word
A Division of WinePress Group
PW

Pleasant Word (a division of WinePress Publishing, PO Box 428, Enumclaw, WA 98022) functions only as book publisher. As such, the ultimate design, content, editorial accuracy, and views expressed or implied in this work are those of the author.

All Scripture quotations, unless otherwise indicated, are taken from the *New King James Version*. Copyright © 1997 by Thomas Nelson, Inc.. Used by permission. All rights reserved.

ISBN 13: 978-1-4141-1480-4
ISBN 10: 1-4141-1480-X
Library of Congress Catalog Card Number: 2009904486

To the needy of the world and the missionaries who serve them.

Contents

PART TWO: THE MAKING OF A MISSIONARY

Acknowledgments

THERE IS NO way we can list everyone's name who has assisted or blessed this calling over all the years we spent as missionaries in Kenya and Uganda. A special thanks goes to Pastor Jack Havens and Mountain Christian Church in Cedar Crest, New Mexico, who taught us how to love Jesus, and to Pastor Skip Heitzig and Calvary Chapel in Albuquerque, New Mexico, who instilled in us the needed biblical knowledge to do a good job in ministry. We wish to again thank all our supporters and prayer warriors for their love for our dear Lord, for us, and for the less fortunate souls we all were serving. We believe we should list some dear brothers and sisters who went more than the extra mile with us from the very beginning, and are still a great encouragement to us in our semi-retirement time.

Sheridan and Soni Fuss have been in our lives from the moment I accepted Christ. Sheridan led me in prayer to be eternally in my Lord's holy presence and service. They were a leading part of our support team, great encouragers, and had the courage to lovingly rebuke us if needed. Their wisdom and love have provided a strength we counted on often.

Donald and Bobby Swaim, Jim and Adelle Kobs, Greg and Nancy Dart, Kerry and Penny Rose, Jesse and Beverly Rich, Will and Lisa Adams, and Walter and Lisa Santiago were instrumental in feeding us the truth of God's Word, encouraging us, and saturating us with abundant love and support. Their frequent letters were filled with tender stories, photos, hang tough encouragement, and assurances of their prayers. Their love for

Christ is an ongoing fire, which kept our zeal very much alive. Like all of our supporters over the years, they are still a big part of our lives.

A special thanks goes to our children, Johnny, Donald (now deceased), Stacy, Stephani, and Shawn, and our ten grandchildren, who saw little of us during the last fifteen years in Jinja.

·A very special thanks to all the Awesome Ugandans on our team. Sunny and I will always be indebted to your loving hearts and unending efforts to save lost souls for God's glory and the growth of His kingdom. Know you are loved and missed.

Introduction to Mission Knowledge

BEING A MISSIONARY is probably one of the most misunderstood positions in the church. Opinions can range from viewing missionaries as some sort of super saints to believing that they just want free trips to visit foreign lands or thinking they are a little crazy to go and work in such dangerous conditions. Maybe a missionary is a little of all the above at times. In reality, though, the Lord looks upon a missionary no differently from the way He looks at anyone else in the body of Christ. God views all of us as servants who should be obeying his or her calling.

Granted, God does give each servant different gifts with which to fulfill the calling He has planned for him or her to accomplish. For example, going to a nursing home to share the gospel requires some very special gifts. These gifts differ from those of the person called to minister to those in jail. Then there are people who minister to those with addictions or run the church bookstore or the Christian radio station or teach Sunday school—the list goes on and on.

God knows the needs of every person and He is busy training you and me to go and take care of those needs. God does not call anyone into His kingdom to just be a pew-sitter, but He has called us all to be servants to one another. There is not one gift—not one—that God has listed in Scripture that is for self-serving. They are all for serving the needs of others. So when you look at a missionary, just remember he or she is only doing what God called and equipped him to do, just as He will call and equip you.

Missionaries Jay and Sunny McLaughlin

This book is meant to help you find your calling, help equip you for that calling, and show you a little of what it is like to live out a missionary calling. You will also see Sunny's and my life during the years we spent as missionaries in Uganda and Kenya in East Africa, as well as gain insight into the technical aspects of missionary work.

This book is broken down into two main sections. The first section, The Life of a Missionary, describes what our life was like as missionaries. The second section, The Making of a Missionary, describes many of the technical aspects of missionary work. There is enough information packed in both of these sections to answer most of the questions you may have about the daily life and technical aspects of mission work. Both sections are necessary for a good understanding of the making of a missionary.

Once you have read part one, The Life of a Missionary, you will better understand the need for the technical portion—part two, The Making of a Missionary. It is very important for you to know the technical aspects of being a missionary before you even attempt to go out. You should also have this knowledge even before you send someone out or support a missionary.

Sunny and I have been lovingly pressured for a long time to write this book—mostly by those who have been our loving and faithful supporters all these years. After having watched us struggle to gain our needed wisdom, they could see how this book would help other missionaries. The benefits include wisdom to protect yourself and the mission from making wrong decisions, leading to possible failures, or even danger, practical knowledge in getting the proper documentation, licensing, and cheaper airfare, and other much-needed information.

What we most hope you will gain is knowledge that will help you do a better job as a servant in what God has called you to do. This simply means that you will end up helping to save many more souls for the eternal kingdom.

The bottom line is that we hope to equip you with information that will help you recognize a missionary calling and go out with much more confidence, ability, strength, and wisdom, in order to do an awesome job in serving others for God's glory.

Now may the dear Lord open your mind and heart, without any fear of the unknown. If we can do this, so can you. We all have the same Father, Who loves you as much as He loves us and will provide for you as much as He provided for us. That, my friends, deserves a big "Amen."

Part One

The Life of
a Missionary

Chapter 1

God Gets an Early Start

GOD IS ALWAYS at work in every Christian's life, from the time he or she is born, until the person dies and goes home to heaven to be with Him in eternity. The only differences are the circumstances and the people involved. As you follow the story of how Sunny's and my life began, notice just how much God was there from the start.

I, Jay, almost did not get a chance at life. I was born in Las Vegas, New Mexico, on April 24, 1938. The hospital I was born in doubled as a sanitarium. I was actually pronounced dead during the delivery, and the doctor walked out of the room. Luckily, my Aunt Rosella was there assisting my mother, and she quickly grabbed me up and began smacking my backside (something the Lord still finds necessary with me far too often!) I began to cry, much to the surprise of the nurses, and was cleaned up and given to my mother. Two weeks later, as my parents were pushing me down the street in my stroller, the doctor happened to walk by. Needless to say, he was shocked to find out I had not died after all and did not send them a bill for his failed services.

My wife, Sunny, was born in Gorman, Texas, on June 2, 1945. She also was born in a hospital that doubled as a sanitarium. So when we say later that it helps to be just a little crazy to be a missionary, you will know that God did get an early start on both of us. We are nuts over each other and about serving Him anywhere He wants.

My family was not wealthy, to say the least. We spent most of our growing up years in an unfinished house with blankets hanging between rooms for walls. My parents saw that we ate and had clothes on our backs. Other than that, however, we did not have much of anything else. Living like this helped me to better understand people of lesser means and their suffering, which I was able to relate to when on the mission field.

My life started with these difficulties, especially through the fourth and sixth grades, when I had rheumatic fever. During the fourth grade, I was bedridden for a whole year and really fell behind my peers. In the sixth grade, I had a relapse and was in bed for another seven months. During this time, I learned how to draw and dream. I fantasized about what the other kids might be doing. When I finally got over my illness, I was much more immature than the other kids, and I lied a lot to try to feel equal to them. Needless to say, that is not an advisable tactic for anyone. I was also extremely skinny. I came out of high school at 6 feet 1¼ inches tall, but I only weighed one hundred and thirty-seven pounds—a mop turned on end. I avoided cracks and strong winds.

From high school, I went into the Navy in 1956 for four years. It was then that I got my first look at other cultures—how they lived and dressed, what they ate, what their houses and transportation were like, and the big difference in the languages. All this excited me very much, especially trying to communicate with them when I did not know their language.

I ended up sounding a bit crazy, slowing my words down and breaking them apart. I did my best and made some nice friends along the way. Little did I know that God would use those experiences to call me to the mission field someday. I have always had a desire to go into other countries and meet new people. God has allowed Sunny and me to meet a great number of people, and we have truly loved every minute of it.

I got out of the military in 1960, and for two years I pretty much wasted my life on worldly living. I kept trying to impress my peers that I was somebody special when I was not. The result of these actions caused me to not keep many friends. Finally, I married a young woman named Linda; this marriage lasted a very troublesome fifteen years. We had three beautiful daughters: Stacy, Stephani (Sam), and Nichole (Nikki). Believe me, I was not the best father or husband in those days. In fact, I was downright awful at it—so bad that she divorced me and moved on with her life. A little later I married again. This marriage only lasted two years and we separated. By this time, I was about as far away from the Lord as one can get. In fact, I did not know about Him at all, except that He had something to do with Christmas and Easter.

My parents seldom, if ever, went to church, but my grandparents on both sides did. What confuses me now is why none of them ever took the time to explain my need for Christ in my life or tell me about what He did for me.

By now I was into about every sickening thing the world had to offer, and I was hunting for more. I was sure if something did not change soon, I would either be arrested or possibly even killed. I was getting more frightened every day, but I just could not stop what I was doing. I came up with a dumb idea that if I could just get out of town, away from the people who were knocking on my life in the wrong way daily, I could change. But that did not work because I was trusting in the same man who was messed up—me.

I did find a job in the country on weekends selling worthless land to poor unsuspecting customers. The owners had one gimmick after another, tricking people into buying this junk. Good old liar that I was, I made some decent money at it, which I am not proud of now at all.

Remember, I said God is at work in everything going on in your life, even out there in the back country. He is at work when you least expect Him to be there, even when you do not know Him at all. When I was out there selling land, I met a couple named George and Sunny.

One weekend, Sunny showed up all by herself and was not looking very happy. I asked her what was wrong, and she handed me a letter stating that George had left her for a much younger woman. He had bequeathed her of all his personal belongings, property debts, and an unfinished house. It turned out that it was all his debts. I thought I would be a nice guy and try to help her through all her troubles. This went on for a couple of months. We became very good friends, and for some reason I did not approach her as I had all the other women I'd met. She was totally different from anybody I had ever been close to before. She was pleasant, kind, and compassionate, and she had very strong morals. It made me really value her friendship.

One day, as we were having a Coke and she was standing with her back to me, she turned around and our eyes met. Suddenly the bells went off, sirens blew, my head swirled, and you name it—it was happening to me. Praise God it is still like that today and even more so. You must have guessed by now that we ended up getting married.

We got married on December 11, 1980. Our children gave us away to each other, Sunny made the cake, and I decorated it. It was a wonderful time. Sunny had Christ in her heart, and it did not take God long to use her to get me into church where I could find Him. A couple of months later, I was in His hands. When I accepted Christ, it was a very emotional time for me—so emotional that I literally crawled over chairs before there was even an altar call.

When God touched me, I jumped at the chance. Then I lay there crying and confessing all the trash that was destroying my life. I gave it all to God to deal with. While I was praying, I kept hearing a voice in my mind saying, "Much will be required, much will be required." I later read it in Luke 12:48, where it says, "To whom much is given, much will be required" (paraphrase). It totally blew my mind. I was so excited, I do not know if it was God Who had spoken to me or not. I believe it was, yet it does not matter. Christ still blows me away in that same wonderful way.

Let me set one thing straight here: I did not become what some people would call a "saint," that is for sure. I still have my struggles and loads of unwanted baggage that God is still dealing with. Yet, God has matured me enough to help reach the lost for Him.

There was a raging fire in me for His Word, and I could not read it fast enough. Reading through the Bible only took me about three months. As you can guess, I did not glean much that way. Then I went back into the Bible and began an extensive study of Scripture, book by book, chapter by chapter, verse by verse, and word by word, until it had sunk in deep enough to begin to be used.

We felt from the very beginning that God would someday call us to serve in some far off place, but "when" was the question. This is a big decision for a couple with a very troubled past to deal with. So we began to pray and ask God to send a missionary to our door when the time was right, when we would be able to go and do whatever He might need us to do. We wanted to make certain that we had enough tools in our "spiritual tool box" to be of some value in a calling and not mishandle His Word.

In closing this chapter, I would like to ask you to take time to review all you have been through in your own life—the good and the bad times. Evaluate those memories and see how much God has been working in your life and what He has taught you through them. Examine carefully to see what you are using and doing for His glory in serving Him and others.

You will find that He has been at work in your life ever since you were born and is continuing even up until today. He will not stop working on you until you are at home in His kingdom with Him for eternity. I cannot say this enough: review until you can see clearly for yourself all of His workings in your life.

Chapter 2

God Does
the Calling

W HY SHOULD YOU take so much time to evaluate all the events in your life? Because if you look deeply enough, you will clearly see God's hands on things you could not have controlled, both past and present, guiding and directing you. These include times to slow you down in order to get your attention so that He can teach you. God also shows His fatherhood through these instructions by motivating you to get your act together when you are sliding either too far to the right or left, heading into some kind of sin.

God knows what is best for you and for His kingdom and will never fall short of reaching His goal for you (Phil. 1:6). We do not know about you, but that is very comforting and encouraging to us. So investigate and seek His will, not yours; you do not want to miss the joy that comes from hitting the mark straight on and being found pleasing in His sight.

Remember in the first chapter, when my wife Sunny and I had placed a prayer before the Lord to send a missionary to our door when He had prepared a calling for us to participate in? Please be careful not to get carried away launching prayers like this, such that you become dependent upon using a "fleece" in everything you try to do. If you are alert and in constant prayer before your Lord, you will become more sensitive to the movement of the Spirit, learning to discern when it is of the Lord and when it is not.

God also can send or place someone in your life whom He will use to bring clarity to any frustration or confusion you might be experiencing.

He did this throughout the Old Testament with the prophets, who brought God's answers and His will to the Jewish leaders in order for them to guide His people. When the leaders followed through on what He shared with them, a multitude of blessings came flowing down upon them. Why? Because of that leader's desire to hear clearly and act strictly upon the will of his God. Maybe you have never taken the time to seek out the Lord's will in the decisions you have made in your life, but, my friends, there is no better time to learn than right now.

Wouldn't you like to feel the excitement that comes when you know you have sought God's will, and He has revealed it to you in some special way, and you have acted upon it in faith, and it has all come to pass as He said it would? That kind of feeling is totally awesome to say the least. You have read about prophecy in Scripture coming to pass, and you believed it as you read it. So why not believe that God can still do it anytime He wishes, be it then or now? God is still the same God, yesterday, today, and all our tomorrows.

Three and a half years went by, and we began to sense that something was going to happen pretty soon. I was doing art murals in the public schools, and in every school I went to, one or more of the teachers—whom I had never met before—would approach me and say things like, "We have this neat video about Africa that I think you might like to take home and view."

Remember, I told you that God is at work in your life all the time to accomplish His will for you and for mankind. God had this happen not in just one of these schools, but in each and every one of them. It was Africa, Africa, and more about Africa. We learned about their cultures, foods, way of life, types of governments, past wars, and accomplishments, be they good or bad. Even a blind man could see God at work in this, how He was preparing us with some foreknowledge of the country that He was about to call us to. We were almost certain that somewhere in Africa was where He would send us to serve. His voice was getting very loud and clear, as everything was pointing in one direction—Africa.

Then one night, about 9:30 P.M., the phone rang. Sunny looked at me, and I looked at her, and we kind of knew even before we answered it that it would be the missionary we had been waiting for. The phone call went something like this:

God Does the Calling

"Hi! I'm Al, and I'm a missionary in Uganda, in East Africa. I understand that you feel God is calling you to be missionaries." I answered, "Yes, Al, that is correct." Then Al said, "Well, I've called because God has work for you to do in Mbale, Uganda, and you will need to travel there in about three to four months. Is that going to be a problem for you?" "No, Al," I answered, "but we will pray and seek God, and our spiritual leadership's will on this before we give you our final answer." Then Al said, "Well, Jay, that is what I would expect of you; just call me as soon as you feel you have an answer from the Lord, be it yes or no." I answered back, "Okay, Al, we will do just that." There was some more talk about the country, about what might be expected of us, the dates, the times, the financial needs, and possible length of stay.

Just a little warning here—the enemy never wants you to do the will of God and will do everything possible to hinder its coming to pass. Sometimes spiritual attacks come from where you least expect them. This calling was to be no different. When we approached the elders of our little church, they had one reason after another for our not going, but none that seemed valid enough to deter us from what we felt God had called us to do. Their main complaint was that we did not have three or four years of seminary training like the apostle Paul had.

I simply could not agree with their interpretation of Scripture concerning Paul's calling by the Lord into ministry. The apostle Paul had been a Jewish spiritual leader as a Pharisee and a member of the Sanhedrin. Paul knew all the prophecies about the promised coming Messiah, but he just did not believe that Jesus was that promised one. It was only when Jesus stopped Paul (Saul) on the road to Damascus that He got Paul's full and undivided attention by blinding him for three days. Later, God sent Ananias to remove the scales from Paul's eyes. Paul, as he is now called, immediately came to believe that Jesus Christ was the promised Messiah.

Please listen carefully to what happened next. It says that Paul went immediately into the synagogue and began preaching Jesus as the promised Messiah. The only reason given in Scripture (Acts 9) as to why Paul's message was not accepted, was the fact that he had been persecuting the church by throwing believers in prison or having them put to death, usually by stoning. The people would not receive him because they were afraid he might just be tricking them and would kill them also. The Apostles took Paul away for a few years, teaching him all they were taught, thus giving

9

the people time to see that Paul's acceptance of Christ as Lord and God was truly real.

With this kind of hindrance, it became difficult for Sunny and me to find any real peace concerning the elders' interference as to whether this was the Lord's will. Consequently, we decided to go ahead and put our house up for sale; we did not, however, tell anyone at church what we were asking for it or the terms that would be involved. We wrote down that we needed $16,000 as the down payment, and that we would carry the balance ourselves at 10 percent, which works out to be about $400 per month. Sounds like a plan, right?

The elders still shook their heads at us selling the house, but we did it anyway. The time was running out quickly on being able to notify Al whether or not we were actually coming. We had not received one offer on the house up until the last month before we were to confirm with Al. Again, at about 9:30 in the evening, the phone rang. Sunny gave me an expectant look—we both thought it likely that this could be an offer on the house. Sure enough, it was a realtor calling with an offer.

Now, look carefully to see if you can see God at work in this. The offer came from two young men, who wanted to give us $16,000 down and have us carry the balance at 10 percent. The payment worked out in the amount of $396.37. We looked at each other and said with a big grin on our faces, "Dear Lord, that's close enough." Do you not agree that only God could have made it happen like this? The elders again turned a deaf ear when we shared what had happened. So we went back to prayer: "Father, what is it we are supposed to do here so that we are in Your will?"

Again, we decided that we would not tell anyone how much the air fare was going to be and leave it totally up to God to meet the need. We sold the house and moved in with a young couple named Mike and Lori, who had a new baby. We were now down to the last two weeks to respond with a yes or no answer. We had been asked to go and share with some other couples and did not get back to where we were staying until our host had already gone to bed.

Boy, did we get awakened to some loud knocking on our door the next morning: "Sunny, Jay, you guys got to get up, we really have something very important to share with you!" You guessed it—Sunny looked at me, I looked at her, and we knew it must be God at work again. See, we needed exactly one thousand more dollars to be able to pay for our airline tickets.

When we came out of our room, Mike and Lori said, "A man called last night, and he believes God has spoken to him in his prayer time and that he is supposed to donate $1,000 to your airfare."

How much more did God have to do to convince our elders that this calling was of Him? "Nope," they said, "we will not agree to send you out." We went home and were really distraught now. Should we go against our elders or not? So we sat down and began praying.

While all these events were going on, and being an artist and sign painter, I had donated some sign work to a new church in Albuquerque called Calvary Chapel. The pastor's name was Skip. So, while we were praying, God touched me with the thought of going to Skip to ask him what he would do in our case. The next morning, I went to see Skip. I walked in and Skip greeted me and said, "You look a little bit down, brother."

I said YES, and that I needed to talk to him. I unloaded all that had taken place from start to finish. When I was done, I asked Skip what he would do if he were in my shoes. He leaned over, placed his hand gently on my shoulder, and said very clearly, "Jay, I would be at the airport with my bags packed—go do what God is calling you to do, whatever it turns out to be." I felt so relieved that I could not help but cry. The peace of God overwhelmed me and I floated all the way home. We got packed and left for Mbale, Uganda.

Chapter 3

Our First Mission Outreach

IF YOU HAVE never had to travel abroad to a third world country, you are in for a mind- boggling experience on your first trip, both going and coming. We had our flight set to take off from New York City, and we had brought a small crate to ship from a port near there to try to save money. This turned out to be a big mistake, as it ended up costing us more by the time we finally received it in Africa. Still, that's the way we started, with a whole lot of zeal and with a lot of ignorance of how to really do things the right way. We should have spent more time seeking advice from those who were savvy about such things, as no books were available.

Then the big day arrived. We departed by air for the first leg of our journey, a fourteen-hour flight into Rome, Italy. When the plane landed, everyone on board started applauding and yelling, "Bravo, bravo." You know what happened next? Sunny looked at me, I looked at her, and asked, "Did we miss hearing about some plane problem or something? They chuckled and told us that it is an Italian custom to applaud the pilot for a job well done. I wonder what the custom would have been if the pilot had announced that there was a problem with the plane—maybe beat the poor guy or throw him out the window!

We were in Rome, and as we had a three-day layover, we took full advantage of it with lots of sightseeing. We visited the Coliseum, lots of ruins, numerous shops, and even Vatican City. I won't elaborate much on that, except to say that we heard a whole lot of bragging about all the expensive artwork they had hanging on the walls and that they had the actual chains that Peter wore when he was in prison prior to his crucifixion. The list goes on and on with great emphasis on how much money it cost.

Another thing I remember very clearly was that most of the people were chain smokers. I had been a heavy smoker before becoming a Christian, and I cannot stand to be anywhere near anyone who is smoking now. As a result, I really suffered in their presence. On the whole, though, we truly enjoyed our visit there and would go there again if we got a chance.

Soon we embarked on another eleven-hour flight to Nairobi, Kenya, to meet up with Al. We landed and it did not take long to find out that things were definitely going to be different in Africa. Visitors were herded in one direction, resident nationals another, charges for this, and charges for that. We endured one delay after another for as long as they could to try to get a bribe out of us by not allowing us to move forward in the line. We did not pay any bribes, so it took us at least two hours longer than it took other people who did.

We proceeded to the baggage counter to try to find our bags and trunks. Finally, after another hour or two, we were able to get them all, and we found ourselves waiting another three hours for Al to show up. We sat in a cold, damp corridor on hard seats. We were tired, miserable, hungry, and fighting feelings of anger for having to wait so long for Al. Like most Americans, if we can't get it or do it right then, we tend to become very frustrated.

Finally, Al showed up with a bunch of excuses, and we headed for his house for a couple of days' rest while we did some much-needed banking. Believe me, banking in a third world country can and will most likely be a nightmare to experience. We finally managed to get the banking completed just in time to load our bags and trunks onto the overnight train for the Uganda border.

The train was actually a very classy old English train with wood-paneled interiors and a very elegant dining car. The waiters were dressed all in white, with white china on the tables, silverware, and a three-course meal included in our ticket price. We had booked a semi-private sleeping quarter in order to keep watch over our baggage.

Sunny and I sat with our noses pressed against the windows, as we did not want to miss anything along the way. There were plenty of poor people

Kenya railways, at Malaba boarder

at every train stop begging for handouts. We found it impossible not to give to the children, who were dressed in rags and had swollen stomachs. We emptied out all the change we carried in an attempt to give each child something with which to buy some food. They all showed so much joy over the blessings God was giving them through us.

If you have never ridden an old train, you might not know what I mean, but you are literally rocked to sleep, so to speak. You actually walk like a drunken sailor for days after you disembark, swaying to the right and then to the left, as you try to move down the street. The train ride was, and still is, a giant memory grabber for us.

Arriving at the border made the airport chaos seem like nothing in comparison. These border agents were highly skilled at making us squirm and wanted us to beg them to let us even get one step forward in the line. There were at least five steps to go through on each side of the border. You may have, at one time or another, asked God to teach you patience. All you have to do is let Him send you out on the foreign mission field and you will learn it, like it or not. I thought we were never going to get to the other side.

After some hours, we were on the Uganda side of the border, where the whole mess started over again. After about three more hours, we were finally finished and could go meet the Ugandans with whom we would be serving.

Mr. Sam Wandendya and his staff were there with big smiles and hugs to match. The first thing they did was to walk up and call me Pastor Jay. I was not yet a pastor, just a servant with a desire to serve the needs of others. It did me no good to try to change this, though, as they informed me that I was now the pastor of Namatala Christian Church in Mbale.

I swallowed hard and said, "Lord, we've got some heavy talking to do about this and whatever else that might lie ahead for us to deal with." His answer to me probably was, "No, you can't do it, but I can do it through you." We all know that nothing catches God by surprise. He knew all this was going to happen and had His plan to get us through it. But He had a lot of convincing to do in order to get me over my fear of failure right from the very beginning. So I cinched up my belt and we took off for Mbale town.

To our surprise, the countryside was very green, with many types of trees, especially banana trees. There were even some small rivers and creeks. It was quite beautiful and enlightening, especially after having just come through all the mess at the border.

Finally, we arrived in Mbale, and we got a truly loud and joyous welcome. The Ugandan people really like to let you know that they are happy that you have come to be with them. They yell very loudly and make a noise with their tongue bouncing up and down in their mouths (ululating), as well as leaping high in the air at the same time. They danced and sang, too. All in all, it was a really wonderful way to initiate a ministry, and it left a lasting memory.

Al had promised Sunny and me that he would stay in Mbale for six months and help train us. Three days after we arrived, however, Al surprised us by saying that he thought we were plenty capable of going it alone, and he took off for Nairobi, Kenya. Later, we discovered that he had a habit of doing dumb things like this, with poor planning, insufficient support, and little to no follow-through on his promises. Sunny looked at me, I looked at Sunny, and we both said, "Yikes, Lord! What's next?" So we took a very deep breath, started unpacking, and began setting up house.

For a couple of months, it went pretty well. We went to many villages, visited town offices and officials, and taught in the church three times a week. They had been telling us that they had many orphans to support and that they had some funding coming in from somewhere in Europe. We had no reason at this time to doubt or question it. Al had painted a walk-on-water picture of this group to us, so we just went along with things. But, as I said earlier, if you are in tune with the Holy Spirit's movement upon you, you will begin to sense if something is not quite right. More and more every day, we were getting the feeling that something was not right.

Eve, Robert, Jay, our Jeep, at the Post Office

We took a few days off and went back to Kenya to do some shopping, as Uganda was still at war within itself. Things we needed were very scarce and too expensive to purchase in Uganda. While in Kenya, we spotted a 1980 Suzuki Jeep with a canvas top. The price was right, so we bought it and headed back to Mbale with everything else we had purchased. It was nice to have our own vehicle to go see more of Uganda, without a bunch of other people tagging along. To our surprise, however, Sam was quite irritated that we had not bought the Jeep in the name of their NGO, Non-Governmental Organization. Later, you will see why he was upset.

In the house where we were living, we had house help, a requirement by the government for NGOs. Their names were Rose and Robert. Rose mainly helped Sunny, while Robert became my right-hand man and did interpreting for me. Robert also did a lot of the cooking, which he really enjoyed. Everything seemed to be going okay; we were staying busy in the office and doing all the church services. We were relaxing a little.

Then we got another surprise from dear old Al, who sent twenty-one interns from the states to stay with us. They just showed up unannounced on our doorstep one day and announced that Al had sent them to stay three weeks, but they had few funds for their food and transport. This was yet another example of Al's failure to plan ahead. To top it off, we had a very old tiny electric stove, about the size of a plastic shipping trunk, and it fried itself on the very first day we tried to feed everyone.

It's hard to imagine what it does to the price of things when things are scarce in a country. Everything has to be brought in or smuggled in from outside the country, and this drives the prices unbelievably high. We had to go and buy a new stove, the same tiny size, and it cost a whopping $800.00. The exchange rate at the time was 3500 shillings to the dollar, and the largest denomination available was 500 shilling notes. Picture this if you can: we had enough money to completely fill this stove, and I had to carry it out of the bank in plastic bags to our vehicle. I looked like a walking armored truck. I then got into the vehicle and drove about two blocks, got out, and carried it into the store. We actually had people follow us from the bank to the store. Sam insisted that the name on the receipt be in his NGO name, which was warning sign number two. Then I literally carried the stove like it was an empty suitcase out to the truck, while the onlookers kept staring. What a rip off—well, "That's life Mwatu" (inside joke, it's a Uganda comedy TV show).

Back at home, we had people sleeping on the floors, in the bedrooms, and in the hall, as we had only two beds in the house. Luckily, they had all brought sleeping bags. We were also facing another very big problem, which was that we only had a small flow of water entering the house. Everyone had to share the same bathwater with three other people on a rotational basis, and the water was dark and full of dirt right from the tap.

One day, everyone got a blessing as God provided a pretty heavy rainstorm, and everybody bailed out under the eaves of the roof to take a fresh clean-water shower. Shampoo and soap suds flew all over the place, but everyone was happy for the moment.

One of the girls in the group had accidentally taken a picture of a police officer, which is a big no-no in any third world country, and he had brought her to my office demanding the roll of film in her camera. She did not want to give it up, as she had some exciting photos she had taken in Kenya, which she did not want to lose. So, I slyly asked the officer if I could see the camera for a minute, went out of his sight, rewound the film, and unloaded it. I knew he would be listening for the rewind sound, so I then got out a new roll and pulled out the film and exposed it. I then went back in with the exposed film and gave it to the officer, who thanked me and left happy. The girl, on the other hand, was crying—that is, until she found out what I had done to save her memory photos.

After all the visitors left, there was a very big void in the house, and, sorry to say, in our pocketbook as well, as they left us almost broke. Things grew a little calmer, and we settled back into trying to do a good job for our Lord and for Sam.

One day, Robert and I had to go to the Catholic mission to get some printing work done. They had the only working printing press in those days. On the way back, we came upon a very large group of people gathered up a side street. Normally, I would just keep on going because there is far too much public circumcising going on in Uganda. They get the person drunk, dance all over the city, and are very disorderly. So my intention was to proceed on home. But the Lord had other plans for me—to turn and go where the crowd was gathered.

When I say the Lord had a plan, I should have also said, He had it all under His control, literally. As I started to drive on by, my steering wheel began to turn in my hands, and we were taken up to where the crowd was gathered. Just having the car turn on its own was mind-blowing enough. Nothing could prepare me for what was happening right in front of me now. As we came to a stop, we could see a large number of soldiers (I believe we counted seventeen) surrounding a young Italian couple; they were beating them with their fists, hitting them with their guns, and kicking them. The young woman was curled up in a ball, and her husband was trying to cover her and protect her from the danger. They were getting pretty bloody, and I could see that the soldiers intended to beat them to death. Being from America, we just don't see things like this being done by our police or soldiers. I could not believe what I was seeing taking place right in front of me.

The next thing I remember was telling my Ugandan helper Robert not to get out with me, because if they saw him with a white man right now, they would kill him as well. As I stepped out of the vehicle, all I remember saying was, "Lord, I'm in your hands." Nothing registered any more about the danger; my mind did not even think about it. I just walked straight in and laid myself on top of the couple. I tried hard to get them to stop screaming and to pray with me. I soon found out in all my feeble attempts at communication that they only spoke Italian. So I began pointing to heaven with my hands clasped together and closing my eyes. I had to do this over and over before they finally got the message and joined me in prayer. As soon as they prayed with me, the soldiers folded back to about ten feet away.

Evidently, what this couple had done while sightseeing was to turn without looking, right in front of a soldier on a motorcycle escorting a truckload of soldiers. The soldier hit the side of their vehicle, flew through the air, and landed headlong into a tree. Everyone thought he was dead, but as soon as we prayed, the soldier rose up yelling and grabbing his shoulder. I am not going to even explore the possibility that he was dead and God brought him back to life, as I didn't even know he existed until everything was over.

It took another fifteen minutes of getting the police to keep the soldiers in line and the couple their much-needed medical help. After that, we headed home. When we arrived and entered the house, Robert began pacing back and forth in the living room. I said, "Robert, it's okay now, we're home and safe." Robert blurted out, "Papa Jay, you don't know what happened."

I informed him that I did know what happened, as I was the one who had gotten out of the vehicle. Robert then came running right up in my face, crying loudly, "Papa, the whole time you were praying over that couple, the soldiers tried to hit you but couldn't, they tried to kick you but couldn't, they even cocked and tried to fire their guns and none of them would fire. They were screaming, I was screaming, but none of the guns could fire."

At this, I went into my room and began shaking heavily all over, from my head to my feet, and crying. Now don't get me wrong, it wasn't over the fear of what had just happened, or the danger we had gone through. It was because, no matter how long you have been a Christian, you will always wish you could see, feel, touch, and know that God is near, that He is really real—that is our human nature. My tears and shaking were because I had experienced firsthand that my God is truly real, and He had touched my life by preventing me and the young couple from being killed. He had brought me to their side to bring them to Him in prayer. God wanted to protect them and show them just how much He really loved them and me. Yes, my friends, our God is very real, and miracles still are available to any of us who call upon His mighty name and truly believe He will answer.

A week later, we were notified that our small crate had come into a port in Mombasa, Kenya. So we traded vehicles with Sam and took their truck for a three-day drive to Mombasa. It took about four days to get the trunk out of port, and we headed back. At the border, we went through more delays in trying to cross back. We did not have the right paperwork to bring it in, but I heard some other missionaries saying that if you stay in their faces long enough and refuse to leave, they will wear down and send you on just to get rid of you. So I did it and it worked.

We had to stay overnight at the border and I had a very bad type of dysentery. There was only one toilet nearby, and it was filthy, with maggots an inch deep crawling on the floor at night. But I could not go in public, so I slid on the maggots as I came in the door to a corner of the room and went, hoping I would not throw up before I could finish and get out. I wiped my feet clean in the dirt and got back in the truck to try to go back to sleep. We had the windows cracked open and hung a tee shirt over the open windows to keep the mosquitoes from eating us alive, and to keep from getting malaria. The next day, we headed out for Mbale.

When we arrived, Rose and Robert were very excited on the one hand, but very scared on the other. When we finally got to sit down and talk, they explained what Sam had been doing while we were gone. He had come into the home and inventoried everything we had—the clothes, furniture, dishes, pots, and pans—everything he could to put on his list. He had also called another mission group in the states and was planning to try to get them to come and take our place. His plan of action was to get us kicked out for some reason or other and take all we had, including our funds and everything he had persuaded us to put in his NGO name. That is why he had been so mad when we had purchased the Jeep without him.

I went to Sam's house and confronted him about what we had, and of course he denied it. He claimed that Rose and Robert had just misunderstood. But not thirty minutes after I went back home, he showed up with four other men and demanded that Rose and Robert come and go with them. Robert and Rose had told us that Sam might try to do this if they told us anything, so I refused. The men started across the room to grab them, and I jumped in front of them and said, "You might defeat me, but you cannot defeat the God Who is going to fight inside of me." At this, they backed down and left.

I went to the police and explained what was going on, and they assigned me a special officer to handle things. He came and I suggested that I call for Sam and his followers to come to our house for a meeting to see if I could get them to admit to as much as I could. The officer agreed. Sam and his people came. I managed to appeal to their pride, and Sam openly shared all his evil intentions—including that they tried again to take Rose and Robert out so they could kill them. I did as I had done before and they left.

When the officer came out of hidding, I asked if he had gotten everything they had said, and he said yes, but that I should remember that he had the last say in the matter. At that time, I didn't know what that meant. It came to mean that whoever pays the fiddler gets to dance. Four days later, I was arrested on the street and taken to the same officer's office. He had informed me not to leave or go anywhere, as I was being investigated. I later found out that this tactic had cost Sam all the corruption money he had stored up in the bank. It was about $8,000, equivalent to about five years' income to them.

While I was purchasing gas the next day, Sam's brother, who did not agree with what Sam had been doing, came and told me that Sam had put out a contract on my life. I returned to the police, and they placed a guard at our house. This is almost funny, as the guard arrived drunk and stayed drunk—big time security, right?

We were desperately trying to obtain Rose and Robert's passports to get them out of Uganda, as Sam was going to kill them as soon as we left—that was for sure. The next day, which was Friday, I went to immigration to try again on the passports, but to no avail. As I was leaving, two police officers approached me and placed me under arrest. They took me back to the office again; this time, Sam, his staff, and our landlord were there. I was being arrested for failure to pay rent. You see, I had been paying rent through Sam's NGO, and the receipts then were his, not mine. So the landlord had joined forces with Sam, and I was going to be bled as dry as they could bleed me. They also produced the list from what they had inventoried in our house while we were gone to Mombasa, and Sam was putting a claim on everything.

We had a lunch planned with another missionary family right afterwards to discuss an escape route and timing. But I had to convince Sam and the crooked officer that we were not leaving right away. So I set up another meeting with Sam and us at the house after church services on Sunday afternoon to go over the list to see what belongs to whom. Yet in my heart, I knew that if we were going to get out alive, we needed to do it as soon as possible. They made me go home and bring the money for the rent that I supposedly still owed. About $3,000 is what they made me agree to pay or else go into the cells, and I had to bring it to them right then. So I agreed, went home to get the money, returned, and paid them. This left us almost broke.

Sunny and I kept our lunch appointment with a seasoned missionary from Canada, named Paul. As soon as I shared the seriousness of our problem, Paul became deeply concerned and made it clear that we needed to leave Uganda immediately. But I said that I had one more opportunity to try to get passports for Rose and Robert and that I needed to do that for their safety. Then we all put our heads together and worked out a plan of escape, including my giving certain signals as to whether I was successful at getting the passports. If I got them, we would all leave together; if not, I would stay behind and distract the guard who was watching our house so that the others could leave without being noticed. The latter also meant they would have to take Rose and Robert to the Quakers' mission on their way to the border and have them hide them there until the passports were obtainable for them to travel.

I was not successful in getting the passports and signaled this as I drove past Sunny and the others who had been waiting for me to come back. This was one of the hardest things for Sunny and me to do, to wave goodbye, not knowing if either of us was going to make it to the border. I headed on to the house and parked in the garage. I then went out into the front yard with Robert and played soccer while waving at Sam's guards up the street in order to keep them from seeing Sunny and the others leaving. After an hour passed, it was my time to take off.

Robert and I finished loading my bags in our little Jeep below the window line so the guards could not tell that I was sneaking off. We locked up the house and threw the keys up on the roof. Robert and I then prayed, and Robert sneaked behind the houses to another mission house, whose inhabitants would then take him to the Quaker mission to join up with Rose. Then I got in the Jeep and drove slowly down the driveway while waving at the guards again, as if I was just going into town again.

Once I got beyond their sight, I turned between some houses so as to stay hidden from the police officer who was near the road I would be taking to the border. I went through gardens, small streams, and piles of garbage before I finally reached my road to safety and then pegged the speedometer as I headed toward Kenya.

When I was passing through Tororo, seven miles from the boarder, a monsoon rain began, and it was coming down so hard that I could no longer see the road. My fear of not making it to the border in time was running high, and I did not want to slow down. So I lifted a quick prayer to the Lord, remembering how He had taken the wheel from me before, and I asked Him to take the wheel again and this time, to drive me the rest of the way. Then I let the wheel go where it wanted to and kept praying as I traveled the last seven miles of a winding road to the border. The rain let up, and I looked up to see that I was about one hundred and fifty feet from my destination.

Suddenly, I began to panic, as I realized that Sunny and the others were nowhere in sight. But just as I was about to head back to find out where she was, they came driving up with luggage and all. I raced to grab her to make sure she was really there with me and was safe. I don't know which one of us feared the other's not making it the most, but it didn't matter now—we both were there and safe. After sharing some quick stories, we cleared the border and headed for Bungoma, Kenya, about a twenty mile drive.

When we reached Bungoma, we quickly unloaded Paul's vehicle so that he could get back to his family. After he left, we found a little place to eat and then went back to our rented room to grab some needed sleep.

About two in the morning, the Lord woke me up, telling my mind that I had forgotten to get the train tickets from Robert during all our chaos in getting out. So I woke up Sunny and our visiting nurse Eve, and we decided that I should sneak back early in the morning, go to the Quakers, and hurry right back. We then went back to sleep, only to be awakened an hour later, being told the police would be at the border waiting for me to cross over. We went back to prayer, and came up with an answer, except this time, I would go to the border, walk out to the halfway point (called no-man's land), and just wait there as I prayed for the Quaker to bring me the tickets.

By now you must be wondering why I did not just make a phone call to have the Quaker bring the tickets. But Uganda was in the midst of internal war and the phones seldom worked. This was one of those times. I got up at about seven o'clock and headed for the border. I arrived and got permission to stand near the halfway mark on the bridge to wait for the Quaker to come. After about thirty minutes of hard praying, I heard footsteps approaching and turned to see the Quaker walking out to meet me. God had awakened him to bring me the tickets, and here he was coming with them.

In my excitement, I started across to meet him, but he placed his hand in front of his stomach, gesturing that I needed to turn around and go back to the Kenya side quickly. I looked over his shoulder and saw behind him four Ugandan police officers hurrying out to try and grab me, so I turned around and headed back. Then I heard the Quaker say, "Jay, you'd better hurry, as they are about to grab you!" Suddenly, five Kenyan police officers came running past me as I stepped onto Kenyan soil, and they stopped the Ugandan officers from grabbing me. I hurried on over until I was behind the buildings, and there the Quaker came to meet with me.

The Quaker quickly told me that Robert had been awakened by the Lord, alerting him to the fact that he still had the tickets that I would need. He also informed me that Sam had been hunting for us all night long with twelve officers armed with machine guns going from house to house. The officers had also taken things from some of the other missionaries, claiming I had hidden Sam's belongings with them. But later, all of them got their belongings back as they had their receipts. The Quaker told me he would have to hurry because they would surely come to his house as well. We prayed, and he headed for his home.

After all this excitement, I headed back to catch up with Sunny and Eve to get them to the train on time. I'm sure you caught the fact that our God can handle anything, and I mean anything. Later that morning, I put Sunny and Eve on the train for Nairobi, with most of the trunks. I took all the other things and started my long drive to meet up with them the next morning in Nairobi.

Finally, we were all back together in Nairobi and were very safe for a change. About five days later, at about two in the morning, we were awakened to some wonderful noise in the parking lot outside where we were staying. "Gross (meaning highly disappointed) Rose, I overpaid the taxi." It was Rose and Robert, who had gotten out safely. They told us that the men came and demanded that they be turned over to them to be taken away, but because they were not in their district, they needed to go get the local police and come back. God took hold of things again and had all the men leave but one, whom they left behind to keep watch over things.

As soon as they left for town, the Quaker got some of Rose and Robert's clothes, placed them on his house help, and covered their heads. They then raced out to his vehicle with the guard watching them, but he couldn't see that it was not Rose and Robert. When the Quaker drove out of his driveway and started up the street, the guard went running down the street after them, but never caught them. The Quaker's wife then took Rose and Robert out the back way to a Ugandan prison nearby. The Quakers had won the prison warden to the Lord the year before, and he hid Robert and Rose there until he could get them their passports. The warden also gave them some money and got them across the border safely.

Not long after all this, we sold our little Jeep and had enough funds to make it home. We left Rose and Robert in good hands, since we had been able to get them jobs with another mission. After some very tearful goodbyes, we left Africa and headed back to America.

When we got on the plane, we were carrying just about as much as we had placed in the hold. We were totally worn out, and the stewardess could see that. Without a word, she took our baggage from us and stored it, then took Sunny and me by the hand, seated us in the first class section, and babied us all the way to Amsterdam, Holland, which was our layover on our route home. Here God was at work again, showing His love for us. We rested up for three days in Amsterdam and had some time to do a little sightseeing. It was a very nice recovery gift from our Lord. Then it was off for home again.

We had sold everything when we were getting ready to go, so now we were headed home with nothing waiting for us and only a few dollars in our pockets. Yet we remembered that God tells us in his Word in Luke 6:38, "Give and it will be given unto you" (paraphrase). So we were not too worried about being in need. What we really needed the most was comfort and reassurance that everything was going to be okay.

A woman's natural focus is "security consciousness" whereas a man's natural emphasis is to "seek and conquer." In Africa, Sunny's security blanket had been ripped out from under her, and God would use that to keep me at home until He had another calling ready for us. That turned out to be another two years down the road and then only after He had touched Sunny's heart and given her the desire to go back. It's always about His timing, not ours, and He knew that I would need to be held back since I had the mission bug now more than ever before.

Let's take a moment to recap what we've talked about so far about being a foreign missionary.

First, God tells us in 1 Corinthians 7:20-24, that we are to remain in "the calling to which we are called" (paraphrase). Now, it is easy to oversimplify this and not leave a job unless something happens and the job is not available anymore—such as being fired or the business going under. I do not think this is what God means at all. What I believe God is trying to show us is that it is more like when you get a feeling inside that you just can't quench. The desire, the drive inside, just won't go away until it comes to pass. I believe God will place a desire in your heart for what He wants you to do, and you cannot put the fire out until you are doing what He has called you to do.

Let me give you an example. You order a banana split with the works on it, and the waiter says, "We're out of bananas and chocolate ice cream—will extra strawberries and orange ice cream be okay?" You know what it takes to make a banana split taste like a banana split, and you won't be satisfied without it being just the way you are craving it. So much so that you will leave that place and hunt it out, and you will not stop looking until you find it and are enjoying every bite of it. I hope this will help you get my point.

God does not give up on anyone He is calling into ministry. He will keep calling you until you finally give up and come. God will place a calling on your heart this way, and then He will make it where you are not satisfied and you don't give up until it does come to pass.

Second, we have seen that God can handle each and every circumstance that comes our way. Remember this, if you really try hard to make sure you are actually doing God's will and you are seeking only to please Him in all you do, He will provide for whatever is needed. He will provide in everything you are doing.

God started by bringing Sunny into my life to bring me before His throne broken and crying out for forgiveness. He then ignited a hunger in my heart for His Word, which still is not quenched. He provided a missionary to tell us where, when, and why we should go. He provided a buyer for our house with the exact amount that was needed. When the church elders wouldn't listen to Him, He provided one who would, who confirmed the calling and told us pack our bags, get on the airplane, and go serve Him. God also helped us feed twenty people with little to nothing in the pantry. He then stopped seventeen guns from firing while He revived a soldier who had been hit and at the same time saved a young Italian couple and myself from certain death. He delivered the needed tickets to the border when we had no way of getting the Quaker a message except through Him. He raised all our funds and the money for our travel tickets, and He kept us safe, all because we were doing what He had asked us to do.

Whatever you do, don't worry if you will have enough to get by on because God will provide completely for anything He has called you to do. Rest assured, He will provide it until it is overflowing into your lap as He promised—whether it's money, food, travel costs, monthly support, or anything else that might come your way. By the time you finish reading this book, you should see the Lord's ability to handle the numerous problems that came our way. My prayer is that this broadens your view of God and His ability and desire to help you.

Chapter 4

Greeted like Failures

WHEN WE ARRIVED back in Albuquerque, some relatives and a few friends from the church greeted us at the airport. We got some hugs and some "Welcome home guys, we missed you, and how was the trip?" But something just didn't seem right to us in the way some of the people were acting. The words they were saying sounded very empty of sincerity, very cold, and kind of distant, and the body language was a bit withdrawn. Their hearts simply were not in what they were saying or doing. We were crying on the inside at what was happening, mainly from what was lacking.

I do not know if I'll ever be able to understand how people can prejudge another person with such callousness, all in the name of the Lord. Here we had just been through one of the most dangerous times in our lives, and we came home to be greeted as if we were failures—an embarrassment to these people. The reason for their behavior soon became clear. Evidently, the church had received a call from Sam, the man who had wanted to kill us for exposing him, telling them that we had caused him to lose most of his support, that we were mishandling Scripture, and that we were teaching false doctrine. He requested that they recall us home immediately, and they agreed. Now how is that for a big welcome home package, when we were totally drained by all we had just gone through in escaping with our lives and doing exactly what God had told us by exposing an evil group of people.

Don't get me wrong, most Christians are very wonderful people, with hearts that are real, loving, kind, caring, and considerate toward others.

Most of those who had come to the airport were the ones who were being real with us, and their kindness kept us from being too overwhelmed with pain and sorrow at the disappointment in the others who weren't so kind. These Christians were the ones who had great excitement at seeing us, wrapping their arms around us to make sure we felt loved and appreciated. The bad greetings at the airport left a bitter taste in our mouths for a long time. In our minds, we kept hearing them say that we taught falsely, that we caused the serious problems we had to go through, and that we should not have gone to the mission field at all, as they had said in the first place.

We are very proud of how well we handled all the issues that took place, and we know that we did exactly what God had sent us there to do. We revealed Sam's evil ways and his false orphan program to his supporters, and we stopped him from killing two of our Ugandan co-workers and ourselves. We are proud to have been obedient to God and not to an evil man like Sam.

God knew that our spirits were way down, and He did not waste any time in making sure that they were lifted back up. Remember, we had sold everything when we went to Africa, and now we had come home empty-handed, with empty pockets and no place to stay. Our circumstances looked pretty bleak, to say the least. However, God had it all taken care of by those who really loved us. They had found out that some of the church members were going to be away from their house for a few months and needed someone to house sit for them. They asked if we would do the house-sitting job. We did, and our loving friends brought us plenty of food, firewood, and extra money to help us get back on our feet.

Just as that house-sitting job was finishing up, Sunny stopped to help a woman whose vehicle had broken down along the highway. Sunny and the woman were having a good time talking, and in the conversation the woman stated she needed to go away for a few months but did not know what she was going to do about her house. Here was God at work again, answering one person's need with another person's need, and both persons being blessed. We moved over to her house and stayed for a couple more months. By the end of that stay, I had my sign work going well enough for us not to starve to death and to be able to rent a place of our own.

Things at the church in the mountains outside Albuquerque did not change much—maybe we just could not forget how we were treated and wrongly judged when we first came home. After much prayer and seeking the Lord, we decided to move into Albuquerque and begin attending Calvary Chapel. This is the church that Skip pastored. The teaching was excellent and brought truth so clearly from Scripture. Skip used powerful passages and related verses to back up everything he talked about. It blessed us abundantly and we continued in our spiritual growth. All we could say after that was, "Thank you, Lord, for leading us to a church body where we can really feel loved, not judged." We are still attending a Calvary Chapel, but now in Corpus Christi, Texas, where we have since moved.

At this point, part of our income was from my artwork. One day, while I was studying Scripture, I thought of how much I would love to see some of these biblical characters in some kind of real life form. I came up with the idea of carving them from jeweler's file wax which is used to create custom jewelry, then make a mold to cast a bronze model. Then it goes back to the foundry to have another type of mold made from that, from which they cast a final product out of high grade pewter.

We began casting these figurines and selling them in Christian bookstores. The hard part was deciding which character from God's Word to do next. We ended up producing twelve different pieces. They averaged in size from two to four inches high, crafted of very high grade American pewter. We were doing well with them until the cost of pewter skyrocketed and they became too costly to produce. This high production cost caused the retail prices to be too high for the public to afford. So we had to pull them off the market. This was another big letdown, as I had poured my heart into each character, as well as into the ones still on the drawing board. "Oh, well! That's life Mwatu" (a Ugandan comedy TV show).

I worked hard to get us fully back on our feet and pay all the bills. We both kept busy serving in the church wherever we could be of use. I attended all the men's groups I could and everything else I could find to increase my knowledge and abilities. Two years later, things began to change when Sunny began talking about going back to serve in Africa.

We started praying about it to seek God's will. While this was going on, one of the members of our family got involved in a very serious crime, and we were all very devastated over it—I do not exaggerate when I say that the whole city was hurting. I went to church to try to see Pastor Skip and discovered that he was studying for his Sunday message. I left a message for him about our prayer need and about possibly going back to Africa. I went back out to my truck and bent down over the steering wheel, crying out to God for help because this burden was really hurting everyone.

Suddenly, I heard footsteps racing up to my truck window. I looked up and it was Skip. He took one look at me, grabbed me in a big hug, held me for a while, and then asked me what was wrong that I would be crying so heavily? I asked him if he had read the note he was clutching in his hand and he said no—it had been handed to him as he was running out the door to catch me. I asked him to please read it, which he did as I waited. When he finished reading, he grabbed me in another big hug, and we both cried for a while. He knew the weight our family must be carrying and the great sorrow we had for the victim.

We prayed for a while and talked some more; then the conversation turned to our possibly going back out. He told me that the reason he came running outside was that, while he was praying over his message, God put it on his heart that I was outside needing help. As he was headed out to find me, he was handed the note I had left for him moments earlier. Then he said he was going to talk to me the next Sunday anyway about two possible mission openings he thought we might want to consider.

Here was God again, already finding the place where He wanted us to serve, even before we had said anything to anyone. One of the missions he shared with us soon faded out because they had closed their base of operations. The other was a youth mission in Mombasa, Kenya.

By now, God had blessed us with much more than we had given up the first time we went out, about threefold plus. After much prayer, we felt led to start selling everything and get ready to go back to Africa.

Chapter 5

The Second Calling

W E DID NOT have the same problem with church leadership this time around since Calvary Chapel knew very well that we had servant hearts, we were strong enough in the Word to do a good job, and we were going to serve others, not ourselves. We had put together a good support team, and were well on the way in our preparations to leave.

Our support team held meetings in which we got to answer many of their questions. They were a little confused, and this gave us a chance to clear things up. Making sure not to leave things in disarray or confusion is very important. Be certain that you know your team has all the details about the calling, the flight times, the arrival dates, and the address where you are going to be staying. Make sure to find out if there is a need for separate addresses for banking, personal, and mission-related business.

You will also need to have your team set aside funds from your support for future travel needs, such as when you come home on a furlough a couple of years down the line or for emergency travel. If your calling is a short-term outreach, you will have to buy round-trip tickets up front and have a return date in place. While on the mission field in a foreign country that is not a part of the American land holdings, you will not have to pay American federal income tax since foreign-earned income is not taxable. If you keep your furloughs shorter than six months, what you receive from your support will still be counted as foreign-earned income, and you will not need to pay taxes on it.

With all this in place for us, we were ready to head out for Mombasa, Kenya, which is on the Indian Ocean coast and a big stronghold for Islam. It is also extremely hot and humid. We had visited Mombasa during our first mission trip and enjoyed it very much.

Here we were in the air again for another fifteen-hour flight, but this time we were routed through Amsterdam, Holland. We came in late at night, and the lights of the city were a fantastic sight. Amsterdam is one of the prettiest places you will ever hope to see. There are wonderful rivers you can take rides on to see many beautiful buildings, gardens, and old style living areas. There are also windmills and shops with wooden shoes called clogs. Their famous pewter figurines and dishware are there to admire. We went to the diamond centers—Amsterdam is one of the diamond centers of the world. We were able to see many wonderful stones and how they were cut from the rough stones to become of great value. Sort of like when Christ calls us out of the world as rough stones,—we are hardened by the world and Christ goes to work on us, chipping away the evil in us and shaping us into the beautiful stones He wants us to be for His glory (Romans 9:21).

All cities have good and bad sides, so not all is bleak, especially if you take the time to look for the good. That goes for people, too. Amsterdam has drugs, pornography, and open prostitution. Yet Amsterdam has some wonderful people who will go the extra mile to make sure you feel loved and welcomed.

Our visit there went by fast, and we found ourselves on another long flight to Nairobi, Kenya. From there we caught another much smaller plane to the Mombasa coast. The possibility of an aircraft crash is always somewhere in your mind when you are flying, and we thought this was going to be it. Just as we were coming in for our landing in Mombasa, no more than a few hundred feet off the ground, we hit what is called a wind shear, which sucks the air right out from under the wings, causing the plane to begin dropping like a rock. Our pilot's abilities turned out to be awesome as he made the right corrections, hitting the power full-bore and leveling out just fifteen feet off the ground, but way too far down the runway to land. Back up and around we went for another attempt at landing, but this time we came in like clockwork. I did like the Italians did when we landed in Rome, and I began applauding the pilot for his great ability to bring us through such a close call.

The Second Calling

As soon as we cleared the airport, we met one of the staff members from the youth mission we would be serving with, and she drove us to the base near the Indian Ocean. We were given a married couple's room in a dorm like building with a bed and bathroom, and that's all. We met the rest of the staff later and were entered into their discipleship training school. Everything went pretty well for a while with the excellent worship times, enough time for our devotions, and time to properly study. Most of the classes were informative, and we gained some new knowledge.

After a month or so, though, we began to notice some very unbiblical teachings we could not accept. I never interrupted any of the teachers during regular class time, but I asked them to please verify their teaching through the Word of God for me afterward. Not one of the teachers could verify his teachings but said, "God has given me this new insight." I read to them from Revelation 22:18-19, where God clearly tells us not to add or subtract from His holy Word because the penalty for this offense is greatly multiplied.

Many other false teachings came along as well, such as, "You must make restitution for every sin you have committed before you are right with God," and "God doesn't know everything except what can be known by man," meaning our lives are just a videotape. Sorry, but my God is all-knowing. The last error that broke the camel's back for us, so to speak, was, "All your weaknesses are demons and need to be cast out." They demonized just about everything. We witnessed them making young people begin to cough, cry, yell, choke, or anything they could think of to get them to do, even passing gas to get their demons out. We refused to have any part of this and called back home to our pastor for his advice on how to handle these issues. He asked us to stay a while longer and document as much as we could.

One morning, the base leader came in and said that "If anyone did not have their outreach portion of their support turned in, they needed to do so soon or else not be allowed to go on the outreach portion of their training." His reason was that the outreach portion was the most expensive part of the decipleship training school, known as DTS.

We had made a decision not to continue with this mission due to all the unbiblical teaching. So we approached that leader the next day and told him we had decided to leave and wanted the outreach portion of the training funds returned to us. His reply was, "Due to the fact that the outreach portion is of such little cost to us, you will not be getting any funds back."

Our answer back to him was, "Sir, you either just lied to us again, or you lied to the whole class the other day, when you demanded they turn in their support for the outreach, saying it was the most expensive portion of their training."

This was the third lie we had caught him in. At our answer, he became furious and left. About two hours later, we were told to come to a meeting with the entire staff in which they all sat in a circle of judgment. Where is that in Scripture? We went as called and were informed that we were not to talk to any of the other students and we had to leave their mission later that afternoon.

I spoke up and told them that God's Spirit was not in their meeting due to their leader's failure to repent for lying to us three different times. At that statement, one of his staff, a girl, spoke up and said, "He is beyond having to repent." Then the leader yelled out, "Give them all their money back—we want no more memory of them, as they are evil spirits."

At this, we left the meeting, and by nightfall we left with all our money returned to us. There were four others who also could not stand any more of their false teachings, and they chose to leave the next day. We had met another couple at a church nearby earlier in our stay who were missionaries and lived nearby. We had been keeping them informed of our situation and what might happen. They let us stay with them until we could arrange to move to Nairobi.

When we arrived in Nairobi, we had a hard time finding a place we could afford to rent. What we finally found was in the outlying slum area, literally. So to the slums we went to set up our house and home. Rose and Robert from our first calling came with their three children and moved in with us. Now we really had a packed house.

One day, as Sunny and Rose, who was very pregnant, were headed out to shop for some groceries, a very drunk lady tried to attack and harm Sunny. Rose, who was a tough lady, quickly got in the face of the drunk woman and scared her off. Thank God.

Finally, we received more funds from home and were able to find a better place to live, something called a "bed setter" apartment near town. That's one large room, a very tiny kitchen, and a bathroom to match. We all moved into it and being "crowded" was now an understatement. We stayed there while waiting on the Lord for His directions. As we waited,

The Slums in Nairobi, Kenya

I signed up at a Swahili school to learn the language. We met some other missionaries and were beginning to settle in.

Christmas was a great time for us and became a great memory. Rose and Robert's kids had never been through an American style Christmas, and we made sure they got one to remember. What we remember most about that Christmas was that all the nationals (Africans) said they did not like eating turkey. When they tasted the way Sunny had cooked it, however, the turkey disappeared as if a bunch of piranhas had attacked it. In fact, Sunny and I only got a small bite of it. We didn't complain since we were blessed to see that they enjoyed it so much.

Late one evening when I was in my devotions with the Lord, He gave me a new vision for us in Jinja, Uganda. The next day, I shared it with our little group, and we all prayed about it for a couple of days. We felt that I should go back into Uganda and share the vision with some local government officials to see how they would react. Remember now, we had escaped from Uganda just two years before and were not sure if it was going to be safe to go back yet. Because they had a new president and new local officials as well, we decided to give it a try.

The Making of a Missionary

The next day, Robert and I headed out for Uganda. We encountered no problems. I got a chance to talk to some of the local officials, and they felt very good about our vision for their people. One official, the town clerk and a very powerful local official, said something to me that really hurt. He said, "Don't be like so many of the other missionaries and just come and build some little church and then live like a king yourself in a big house and end up doing little to nothing for the poor people of Uganda."

This hit deep inside me and has never been forgotten, and it has affected all of our mission planning in Uganda. When we got back to Nairobi, we began planning our return home, where we would wait on the Lord's timing as to when He wanted us to go back to Jinja, Uganda and begin the work of fulfilling the vision.

Once we were able to get Rose and Robert work again with other missionaries, we departed for the United States and home. This time, our arrival was what we would expect it to be—a very heartwarming time. There were lots of hugs and kisses and old teary Jay did a lot of crying on everyone's shoulders because I was so happy to see everyone and feel such love being poured out on us.

Each time we had gone to Africa, we had sold all we had and put it into the work of the Lord, to share with those whom we would be serving. Please don't think we didn't have our moments when we had thoughts of holding a little back for this or that! But the conviction we felt inside won those thoughts over, and we waited on the Lord to provide for us. Again, I will say it, "You cannot out-give God, not ever." This time we had given up a house, two vehicles, and a motor home, three times more than we gave up on the first calling.

We settled back in, and I started my sign and art business back up. We bought two wrecked vehicles from a salvage lot through the help of my dear dad, since deceased. One was a station wagon, and the other was a pickup. My dad had taught me how to do some body work as I was growing up, and I put that training to work rebuilding the two vehicles. Eventually, we had two affordable pieces of transportation. Meanwhile, I kept thinking that the Lord might send us back out in just a few months. I had also asked the Lord not to send us back out until we had enough tools in our spiritual tool box—tools of biblical wisdom and abilities to fulfill the calling He had given us. Things were headed in the right direction now, so we just held tight to our trust in God's timing and will.

Chapter 6

God Does all the Training and Equipping

WHEN WE LEFT Kenya, I had this big idea that we would not be home more than three months. I wanted to get right back and get the vision God had given me put into action. But God had other plans, and He knew I needed more training and equipping before we would be ready to meet what it would take to fulfill the needs of this calling.

After three months went by, then five, it became obvious that God had a different plan from mine. God was also using somebody else to hold me back, and that was my wife, Sunny. God knew I would not pressure her to go back and that Sunny would tell me on her own if she felt it was time to go—and right now was not the time. Sunny had had her security blanket ripped out from under her in the previous two callings, and she was not willing or ready to go back. I accepted that because I knew it was from the Lord. God is the one Who controls each of our steps, and it is best to wait upon Him, and not trust just in yourself.

We went back to prayer and asked God not to send us back until we were both equipped with whatever He wanted us to have in the way of knowledge, abilities, training, and support. We wanted to make sure the timing was of the Lord, just like it was in the other two callings. For that reason I asked Him not to send us back out until our pastor, Skip, felt that I had grown and matured enough to be ordained a pastor. I even went a step further and did not ask or tell them to train me for this calling, and left it to the Lord. I also asked God to have the church leaders be the ones to come and ask me to join the training programs He wanted me in, without my asking first.

I started my sign business back up, got a bunch of clients, and began working hard to make ends meet. We had little to nothing again when we arrived home, and we had to start getting our act together from scratch. Before long, God had given us back more than we had given up. Like it says in Luke 6:38 and Matthew 19:29:

> Give, and it will be given to you; good measure, pressed down, and shaken together, and running over will be put into your bosom. For with the same measure that you use, it will be measured back to you.
>
> —Luke 6:38

> And everyone that has left houses, or brothers, or sisters, or father, or mother, or wife, or children, or lands, for my name's sake, shall receive a hundredfold, and inherit eternal life.
>
> —Matthew 19:29

These verses teach us that we cannot out-give God since He will give it back overflowing into your laps. We were not rich, yet we had two vehicles, we owned a house, our bills were being paid each month, and we were eating just fine. God is so loving toward His children and knows far better than we do what we really need, that He only gives us what is best for us.

I began serving as an usher twice a week at church and then became head usher. I also worked patrolling the parking lot for a while and washed the kids' toys. They also asked me to join the counseling training program, which ended up being five different training classes, and then I began counseling after services. I was asked to go through kinship leader training and then start a kinship in our home. Finally, I started training new kinship leaders.

Sunny was growing as well. She was busy going to the women's training seminars and retreats and helping run the tape room. We were both enjoying having some unpressured time together for a change. I guess God knew we needed some long-term rest from all the rough times in Africa during the last two callings. Yet God was using those difficult experiences as part of our new training for the future work He had planned.

Three years had now gone by and I was beginning to wonder if I had heard God correctly. We moved into the house we bought and were really settling into the everyday events. The kinship we started in our house had grown now to thirty-eight people every Thursday night. We made a lot of new friends and had the joy of watching many of them go on to become strong servants in the church.

God was busy training me in ways I would never have thought about or been able to gain on my own. Next came the more serious leadership training classes. More counseling followed, and I had new kinship leader training to do. Some form of training was coming at me all the time. However, the thing that came my way that really woke me up was when Skip asked me to start coming to the pastor and leadership training classes. You know I turned him down, right? Actually. I jumped at the chance for more training. Just because you go through these classes does not make you a pastor—that is strictly God's business. The pastor classes were extremely good because Skip is a great teacher, and I was able to glean much from him. Week after week, I could see why God had me stay home so long. He had shown me how much it takes to become a mature spiritual leader, let alone a pastor.

Skip's teaching placed me back in the Word deeper and deeper, until I thought I could not learn any more. Then he would send us right back in there for more. I loved it because I was growing as I'd always hoped I would someday. I began to notice that when I was up front counseling after services, I was sharing Scripture with a lot more confidence than ever before. The training was paying off in more abilities and, hopefully, in more maturity.

A couple more years went by, and we had now been home for about five years. There is a big difference between that and the three months or so I had originally expected it to be. It was at this time that I was asked to do a special worship night on Wednesdays. I do not sing very well or play any instruments, but I was given the responsibility to see that everything was kept biblical and orderly. That night became one of the most blessed times I have ever spent before the Lord in worship. The Spirit moved so strongly each time we got together. It was nothing wild or crazy, just honest, heartfelt worship of our King.

But soon the worship band's lead singer moved to another state, and after that things just were not the same. Within about a month I had to shut the whole thing down. Yet the memories will always be there to bless me when I feel a little downcast.

About mid-1990, things started to quickly come together. As Sunny and I were sitting down to dinner, she turned to me and said, "Honey, I think God is telling us to consider going back out to Africa."

I almost choked on my food because I could hardly believe what I'd just heard. All I could say was, "Thank you, honey, for loving me and our Lord so much." I went to bed that night floating high, and thanking God for giving me such a godly and loving wife and a new hope that the vision just might come true after all.

Another month went by, and I was busy serving everywhere in the church that I could. I remember a young man with a bent arm from polio as a youth who came up to me after service for some counseling. He was asking for prayer about a job interview he was to have later in the week, and he had been out of work for a good while. His financial situation was pretty bleak. I took his hands in mine, and we began to pray.

As we prayed, I felt his arms move about, but I continued on. Suddenly, he pulled loose from me and began jumping up and down, yelling, "My arm is straight, my arm is straight!" He ran back up to me and showed me his arm. God had straightened it out while we were praying. I had never experienced an instant healing miracle like this before, and believe me, I was extremely happy for him.

Later in the week, he came up and told me that he got the job. They had told him they were considering possibly not hiring him due to his physical handicap, yet when they saw that it was no longer a problem, they hired him. Praise be to God, Who loves us so unconditionally.

The big day I had been hoping for arrived. One Sunday after services, I had just finished counseling with five different people and was sitting on the steps resting my thoughts, when the Assistant Pastor, Gino, came up and sat by me. This guy loved to play jokes on people and was good at catching people off guard so they didn't see the joke coming.

He stated to me very gruffly, "Jay, Skip wants you in his office on Thursday—he has something bothering him that he wants to discuss with you." At this, my mind went wild trying to think of what I might have done that had made Skip so mad at me. Gino went on to play it for all it was worth. Then he said, "It's been bothering him so much lately that he knows he must do something about it before it goes on much longer."

Now he really had me worried, and he could see that I was getting very concerned and too downcast for him to let it go on any longer. So he said, "Jay, are you ready for this?"

I said, "Ready for what?" Then he told me that Skip was not angry at me at all, but that what he really wanted was for me to be in his office on Thursday so he could ordain me as a pastor.

At this, I exploded in tears of joy, and then it hit me hard what he had just said. A sudden fear came over me; being a pastor is a giant responsibility, and people really expect you to know what you are doing and saying. I asked myself whether I was really ready to become a pastor. Satan never lets up trying to discourage us or make us too afraid to do God's work. He can make us feel so incapable when we look at our own abilities instead of looking at and knowing God's abilities.

God always knows best, so I began to relax a little and took off to find Sunny to tell her, "It's time."

"Time for what?" was her response.

I said, "Time to go back to Africa—Skip says he wants to ordain me as a pastor."

At that, we both cried a little and went home. We spent a long time with the Lord in prayer of thanksgiving and asking Him to help, help, help us to be strong and do a good job.

Later I asked Skip exactly what time he wanted me to come in, and he said to bring Sunny and come to his office around 2:00 P.M. on Thursday. Sunny and I showed up on time (as if I would be late for this!) and went into his office, where we were greeted by his staff and the elders. A man named Rick, with whom I had gone through many of my classes, was to be ordained as well.

Skip began by saying how he had watched God take the two of us from our basic foundation and begin to build two godly men on top of it—how we served without complaining and were willing to go the extra mile at any time, and on and on. By this time, I was getting a little weak-kneed and dizzy since I did not see myself the way Skip was stating things. Yet God had called us there that day to become pastors and leaders in His callings wherever they may be.

Then everyone gathered around and laid hands on us. As we prayed, I got the same fear I had the day Gino told me about being ordained. *This is a big responsibility, Jay,* I told myself, *are you sure you can handle this?*

God reassured my heart by allowing me to feel and see that it was not I who had to handle things; it was Jesus working through me who would accomplish whatever came my way. I just needed to stay prepared and willing to do whatever he placed in my path and share His Word.

After many hugs and encouragement all around, Skip said, "Go and do what God is putting on your heart to do, and do it well for His glory."

Those words have rung in my ears quite often as we served over the years. They have helped me to remember why I needed to keep studying hard because you never know what He has in store for you just around the corner. If you fail someone who is seeking God, you have failed to do what God brought that person to you for, and that is to fully reveal His Son Jesus Christ to that person.

Being scared may sound a little childish to you, but if you are not just a little scared of failure, you might be getting overconfident in your own personal abilities and not relying on God during the rough times that come along. I do not fear the Lord like you would fear a lion. I only fear failing Him, resulting in giving the enemy the glory and not the Lord. God says in 1 Corinthians 10:13:

> No temptation has over-taken you except such as is common to man: but God is faithful, who will not allow you to be tempted beyond what you are able; but with the temptation will also make the way to escape, that you may be able to bear it.

This verse indicates that He will not give us more than we can bear, but in the midst of it, He will provide a way out. We just need to be more trusting in Him and His Word and less in ourselves.

Later, you will hear, and I hope feel, His great power at work in all the awesome events that unfold before your eyes in what He allowed us to go through. Like the events from the previous callings, the following events took place during our service in Jinja, Uganda, for the last thirteen years before returning home.

Chapter 7

All Cracked Up, but No One is Laughing

SOME THINGS DO not always go as planned, or as well as you hoped they would. Knowing that, and adding the fact of being in a third world country, you can be sure it will multiply many times over.

We left America on February 1, 1990, and flew another fifteen-hour flight to Amsterdam, Holland. After a few days, we flew to Entebbe, Uganda. Overseas flights are always long, and this was one of them—fourteen hours of restless sleep, three movies, lots of reading, studying, and eating those wonderful in-flight meals…hmmm. Arriving in Entebbe was a rude awakening for us.

What a difference there is between America and a war-torn third world country like Uganda! We got off the airplane to be greeted by an air terminal riddled with fifty-caliber machine gun holes. The inside was the same—bullet holes everywhere. It gave us an eerie feeling that kind of crawled up our backs and then knotted up our stomachs.

We entered the receiving area to find five long lines, which left us trying to figure out which one we were supposed to be in. We finally spotted a sign indicating a line for nonresidents and got in place for a forty minute wait. At least it did turn out to be the right line.

After the first step was completed, we moved on to another line to get our entry visas and then to the line at immigration. Both areas had some very deliberate holdups while they tried to get us to pay a bribe. As a result, it took over two hours to get everything done. Getting our bags took a very long time, too, because we were not there when they came off the airplane and were delayed by the workers angling for their bribery money.

After almost three hours, we were finally heading out of the airport, looking for transportation to Jinja. We found two old cars that were used for taxis. After some very hard negotiating, we came to an agreeable price and headed out.

We had arrived at Entebbe eighteen hours earlier than our scheduled arrival time. Robert and Rose were in Jinja, and we had no way of contacting them to let them know we had arrived. We didn't even know where they were living, and the phones were not yet working. Even if the phones had been working, Robert and Rose were too poor to have one. We worried about not being able to contact Robert and Rose on our way to Jinja. Fortunately, our drivers knew Jinja pretty well and took us to a decent hotel to spend the night.

We got some much-needed rest and got up early to figure out how to find Robert and Rose. We told one of the workers at the hotel about our problem, and he suggested that I go to the local market center and stand there since this was where the post office was. It was also very near the taxi park where Robert would have to go to catch a ride to Entebbe.

I checked with the post office first to see if they had an address for Robert and Rose, but that did not pan out. I then went outside and watched everyone go by. After about thirty minutes, I spotted Robert a block away, headed for the taxi park. I started yelling as I ran to catch him. He finally heard me, but he was having a hard time finding the source of the yelling.

At last, he spotted me and came running, jumping into my arms and almost knocking me over. He was so excited that he was laughing and crying all at the same time. I think he was a little happy to see me. After we finished our greetings, we went hunting for a small truck to rent. We went to pick up Sunny and all our baggage and headed for the house they had rented for us.

Rose saw the truck coming down the road and came running toward us with her Ugandan greeting, complete with some very shrill tongue waggling and screeching sounds you will not soon forget. I think her yelling came pretty close to breaking what few windows were left in that area. She grabbed us up, hugging us almost to death—she is very strong, as are most African women.

All Cracked Up, but No One is Laughing

There was much crying, due to everyone's happiness at being back together after a separation of over five years. I think they were considering renaming the street "Tear-Jerker Lane," instead of First Lane.

There is a reason I called this chapter "All Cracked Up, but No One is Laughing." When things quieted down, Sunny headed for the house, came to a screeching halt, turned, and looked at me, saying, "Jay, come see this."

I hurried over to her, and she pointed to the front of the house. Lo and behold, there was a crack all the way across the front of the house big enough to stick my hand in. That was the first of many "Jay, come here's" she yelled at me that day. She opened the front door and another "Jay, come here" came whistling my way. The place was filthy, with dirt all the way up the walls and all over the floor. It was painted some kind of yellow buckskin color, I think. Sunny bumped a door as she went to go through to another room, and the cockroaches ran down out of it like water overflowing from a bathtub.

"Jay, Jay, come here."

"Yes, honey, I'm coming."

This happened with each of the doors—cockroach villas for sure. She then went into the so-called kitchen; it had no sink, no stove, no refrigerator, and no hot water heater. It was so dirty we had to kick things out of the way just to get in. "Jay, come here; Jay, come here." Boy, she sure knew my name that day.

We proceeded to the bathroom, where both the sink and toilet were broken in two and had been clogged up for who knows how long. You guessed it, "Jay, come here," came rolling out again. I found a water tank on the roof that was also broken and it was too small to accommodate the number of people who would be staying there. Sunny came up to me and said, "Honey, what have we gotten into here? What are you going to do about this mess?"

All I could say was, "Honey, give me about two weeks and I will have it livable for you."

"Two weeks maximum is all you're going to get, fella," she said and then smiled at me with one of her very precious Sunny looks that just seem to melt me into submission.

"Okay, baby, okay." What else could a guy say after that smile?

When a country is as war-torn as Uganda was, we couldn't just run down to the local hardware store and find what we needed. I spent days trying to find the parts and equipment to get the house even started on the road to repair. When I found anything, the price was extremely high due to its having been brought in from outside the country. This time-consuming effort produced the sinks, toilet, paint, and some rebar with which to mend the front of the house. We finally found some screen wire to keep out the mosquitoes, flies, and tons of other creepy bugs and lizards.

The water tank could be made into a sort of hot water tank by painting it flat black to absorb the sun's heat during the day. Robert went in search of paint and came home with some about four hours later, very tired from walking up and down, looking in every shop he could find. We made a bathing schedule for us to follow, as to who gets the warm water bath that day to bathe with and who gets the special blessing of the good old cold water bath instead.

The front of the house was a totally different job to do because it was so badly damaged. We ended up making what looked like giant staples out of iron bars, then drilled holes in the brick wall so we could insert the iron staples into them. We also got some big timbers to brace and press the front wall tightly together. Once we had everything in place, we inserted the staples and cemented it all together.

After a couple of weeks, we were surprised that our efforts actually worked out, and it held together just fine. We then concentrated on sealing up the many leaks on the roof we discovered after the first big rainstorm. Finally, the work was completed, and Sunny could quit yelling, "Jay, Jay, come here." She said to me, "It looks like we've got ourselves a home to stay in." We went on to have many great memories while living in that little old house.

Something I forgot to mention was that we made a deal with the landlord to allow us to spend half the money for rent on repairs and give the other half to him. He was very happy that we were so willing to do the work and that he would end up with a nice-looking home someday and could rent it for much more money.

Sunny and I walked close to five miles a day searching for food items, let alone all the other stuff we needed. The marketplace was where we got most of our vegetables, fruits, and meat. Buying meat in those days was a sight to see, and an experience we did not soon forget. The meat was kept hanging on a hook out in the open air all day long, with flies swarming all over it. Sunny picked out the part she wanted, and they would throw the side of beef down on a big wooden stump. Then they would take a machete and whack off a kilo or two. They wrapped the meat in a banana leaf and handed it to us, flies and all. We mostly bought what is called the fillet because it is located deep inside the ribcage where the flies can't reach easily and was more tender than other cuts. People could also buy other interesting protein sources, such as white ants and grasshoppers.

Typical meat market, notice the Machete

After we grew more comfortable living there, we began making plans to start all the required paperwork. We needed to get our NGO license in place. An NGO simply means, Non Governmental Organization. This license must be in place before you can do any kind of ministry or other type of work. Until that time, you are just a visitor in their country on a visitor's visa. To stay and do ministry, you must get a "Work Permit," and you cannot get it without having your NGO in place. You also have to keep paying the big bucks on visitors' visas until the NGO license is obtained. Therefore, it was very important for us to get this part taken care of as soon as we could. We were introduced to a very godly Ugandan lawyer named Peter Nyumbi, who worked with us on getting it done right. Peter went on to become an important part of our Board of Directors and was always a blessing to our ministry while we were in Uganda.

Like I said before, bribery is rampant in everything you have to do. Remember, though, that you must never pay it because when you do, the amount demanded will just grow bigger and bigger every time you return to get something done. The bottom line is, don't pay a bribe at all.

A Baptist missionary once told me the best way to handle it is to just wear them down. You do this by standing in their face, in front of their desk, until they give in to your need and sign your paperwork. They will tell you to leave, but you just play dumb and keep asking for what you want. Do not give up; they will eventually give you what you want just to get rid of you. It does work, as most of what we got accomplished was done this way.

I will say this—sometimes it takes a month or so to get the victory, but the next time you come to their office, they will get it done much quicker. The main thing to remember is that you are giving the Lord the victory, not the enemy.

Another problem we faced in every office is that there are few or no phones; the ones you do find will probably not be working because the phone bill was not paid. Because of this, you cannot call ahead to make an appointment and will have to go there physically. Another problem that will likely arise is that they will seldom be in their office to do any work. Consequently, you have to go back day after day until you finally catch them. Still another problem is that very seldom will one office be near the other you need to visit. As a result, you will end up walking back and forth across the city, miles this way and more miles the other way. I did this week after week after week until it was all finished. This process took me close to a year to get it all finalized. I believe I was in the best shape I had ever been in years.

As soon as the NGO license was in place, I started the same process to get the paperwork completed to have our container shipped from the states to Uganda. This took another year of hard work, much walking, and an awful lot of frustration, learning more about being patient. In addition, the container was not even shipped for a couple more years since we did not have a permanent location for it. While I was working on the container, I was also trying to obtain our work permits so that we could get the whole ministry going.

Remember what I'm sharing with you here, and do not forget it—we Americans are used to getting things done fast, and when that does not happen, we become very frustrated quickly. But that simply does not work in a third world country. If you become angry at them, you will likely create a disaster for yourself, which you will have to mend later, if you even can.

You receive a calling from God to go out and win souls for His kingdom and His glory, and when you arrive you will want to rush out and get your feet all wet. But you cannot put the cart before the horse, so to speak. If you do, you might find yourself without your needed paperwork in place, and then you might even be asked to leave the country. When this type of thing happens, you will have left a very bad Christian witness and become a poor steward of the calling God had given you. Sure, it is not easy to endure all the garbage they put you through, but please remember that Christ went through some pretty tough garbage during His ministry, and so will you.

There are many things you have to get put in place that you don't even know about yet—things you don't think about while you are so excited at home, preparing to go out. Some of them I have already shared with you, but there are a few more items you should put in your "Things-I-must-know-about tool box" to do the work you are being called to do.

Here are just a few of the necessities you will need on the field:

- a mailbox and number
- a drivers license
- different types of insurance
- a house to rent
- possibly land to build on

In addition, taxes must be dealt with, work permits must be considered, medical issues will need to be addressed, language(s) might need to be learned, and meeting the local officials will be necessary. These are just a few examples of the many things you must consider prior to going out. The rest are in Part Two of this book.

Meeting the local officials is an absolute must. Not doing so can and will cause some of your paperwork or request to backfire on you when you really need them. Examples include when you are trying to obtain land, trying to build, or needing a special permit to do an outside ministry, such as a crusade. You will especially need an official should you get into some kind of legal difficulty, which I can pretty much guarantee you will somewhere down the line.

Here is a story on the lighter side of things, which took place right in the middle of all my hard work trying to get things put in place. One day, I came home very tired and hungry, and when I walked through the door I noticed the dinner table had been completely set. I also noticed that everybody's plates had hamburgers on them, yet there were no buns, nor had anything else been placed on the plates. When I looked at mine,

Large juicy White Ant, Yummy

however, it was completely made up and ready for me to eat. So I excused myself to go wash my hands before eating. When I came back out, Sunny was standing at the other end of the table with a video camera on her shoulder, and everyone else was staring at me and trying not to smile. A little light went off in my head at this point. The previous night, we had been awakened by our neighbors banging cans and bottles on our porch in an attempt to collect some flying white ants.

We had the only working porch light, and these white ants were swarming around the light. The sight was exciting to watch, as some of the people were eating the ants as they were catching them. Remembering this, and figuring that they must have placed some ants on my hamburger, I made a decision. I decided that if I was ever going to get brave enough to eat any ants, this was the best time.

I sat down and slowly lifted up each layer of my hamburger, looking underneath to see if there were any ants. By the time I went through the lettuce, tomatoes, onions, mustard, ketchup, and pickles, I finally got to where the ants were hidden. They had placed about twelve ants on it, and they were fat and juicy-looking, yet very cooked. Everyone was now laughing and hoping to see me take a big bite. I decided this had to be the time for me to grab my first white-ant sandwich since it was so well masked with all the other goodies. I slowly raised the sandwich to my mouth, grinned really big, and took a great big bite.

As I did, all I could hear in unison was, "Oh, gross, Jay, gross!" Robert and Rose yelled, "You're a true Ugandan now, Papa Jay."

Ugandans also eat green grasshoppers, but that is where I draw the line on exotic food. I could never get over the splattering of their guts on my windshield.

Let's look back to our earlier days, when we finally needed a van to get things done. Having to walk everywhere was interfering with our work schedules. Everyone, including the team back in America, began praying over our vehicle need. By the time two weeks went by, the money had been donated in the exact amount we were praying for and that was $4,500. We had found a four-year-old Nissan van, with only 18,500 miles on it that had just been shipped to Africa from Japan.

If I have heard correctly, Japan does not allow any used vehicle to remain in the country more than four years; after that, it must be shipped out. When there are enough of these vehicles stockpiled at the dock, third world-country buyers come in and place bids on them. Only third world countries are allowed to purchase these vehicles, via a United Nations agreement. When you purchase a new vehicle in Japan, you also pay for the disposal of your old one at an established cost, which is credited on your purchase. Our van was still like new inside and out. God really blessed us with it. That same little van is still working for the mission today.

Now that we had some decent transportation, we could finally go and see what some of the rest of the country we were serving in looked like. We soon learned that the main cities were about seventy-five years behind the times, that is, compared to America. But the deeper you went into these villages, you could see that they were from two hundred to four hundred years behind modern day progress. In many places we went, the people had never even seen a white person and came running up to see if our white skin would rub off. One time a woman started playing with the hair on my arm and progressed on upward to some hair sticking up out of my T-shirt top. I finally had to say, "That's far enough, madam," and then remove her hand gently from my neck.

Some other places we went had never seen a vehicle before and were highly amazed by it; they could not stop touching. Most of the living quarters were made of sticks with mud covering them, with a thatched grass roof. They mixed mud and cow dung to make a plaster-like substance, and then plastered the floor with it. You could smell it oh-too-well as you entered to visit.

One time, Sunny had a small mirror she had taken out to get something out of her eye, and one older woman saw it and became very inquisitive about it. So Sunny showed this lady what her own faced looked like. The lady started laughing and jumping up and down, as she had never seen her own face before. Then she took the mirror and went running around showing all the other women what they looked like. We Americans have sent men to the moon, and yet these people had not even seen a mirror. The sight that day was one to cherish for a long time.

Another funny story happened when we went to a village school to give away some clothes and hotel soaps that were given to us. I thought I had a good plan for giving them without any real problem, but that was short-lived. When I started handing the soaps out, things were going okay. However, because these people do not have much of anything, they began to worry they were not going to get one and began pressing in all around and grabbing at me. I started backing up while handing the items out, then I was walking really fast, and finally I was on a dead run, throwing them over my shoulder to keep from being trampled by a few hundred children. Sunny was taking pictures and laughing at me so hard she could barely stand up. I have to admit, it must have been a funny scene to watch.

We also wanted to hand out some clothes, and as we were leaving the school, we came upon a woman with a girl who was wearing few clothes. We stopped, and as we were getting out, the thirteen-year old girl took off running away and crashed straight into a thorn bush, embedding herself deep within its thorns. We tried to coax her out, but she kept wiggling deeper in. Her mother just laughed and watched. Then she went away and got another daughter, who was about ten. This child was so skinny that as her mother held her up in the air, out of her private parts worms were dropping like sand in an hour glass. We were devastated at the horrible condition of both of these children's health, and the mother was just too ignorant to notice. We gave the mother some of the clothes for each girl and quickly left, hoping the girl in the bush would come out since she was so afraid of us. Their fear is due to how the early British used to beat, whip, and sometimes hunt them as if they were just game animals. We saw the factual details of this in the Kenya Museum of History.

Chapter 8

Growing Pains from Within

THE HOUSE ON First Lane, where we had been living since we had arrived in Jinja, was quickly getting too small for the growth that was taking place. The church that was meeting there could no longer fit in that small house, so we started looking for a much larger place.

One big problem, though, was we still did not have much support coming in and needed to be careful not to overburden ourselves. Yet we knew that if God was causing the growth, then He also had a plan to meet that growth, and all we needed to do was go out in faith and put it into the Lord's hands.

We began by looking at every possible location and then investigating what it would take to get each one. We had to trust in the Lord to increase our funding to match. We finally found a very large five-bedroom house that was not finished inside or out—no ceiling, plumbing, electricity, windows, or doors, and nothing was painted. The house was the perfect size we needed, but what could we do to make it livable should we get it? Where was the money going to come from?

I met with the owner and began getting her interested in considering leasing it to us on special terms. She was a born-again Christian lady named Angela. After the whole team spent quite some time in prayer, seeking God for a way to follow through on this house, we pooled our thoughts and put a plan together to approach Angela to see if she would accept.

The plan would allow us to pay her half on rent and the other half would be put toward finishing the house on a five-year lease agreement.

After much debating, with her trying to get more out of us, she finally gave in and agreed to our offer of $230 a month. Half went to her, and the other half was used for the house repairs, with receipts to verify our purchases and progress.

The first thing we did was put in the windows and doors so we could keep the mosquitoes and thieves out, and to prevent us from getting more malaria. Then came the job of putting in the wiring, plumbing, sinks, toilets, and tubs. We also needed a good stove and refrigerator and a large dining table and chairs. We would also need seven bunk beds, as teams were planning to come out for periodic visits.

One of our biggest undertakings was finding a large enough water tank to serve a household of eleven to forty people, all coming at different times. We finally found a 350-gallon water tank with the tower to place it on, and we purchased it. Raising the whole assembly into position was a major job, and it took about ten people pulling and pushing to get it standing upright. Yet with some old backyard ingenuity, we managed to get the job done.

We also had to repair the fence around the property to give us some protection at night from all the thugs who roamed throughout Jinja and were very desperate for money on which to survive. Every night, they moved around the city seeing whom they could rob, and many of the other missionaries had been robbed. We had searched out and bought some very big and strong guard dogs to keep these thugs at bay, and the dogs did their job. Most Africans fear big dogs very much, especially if they are black dogs. This is because the witch doctors tell the people that such black dogs are demon dogs.

Finally, the big day came when we could actually move in. We had still not painted the walls, and we had bare concrete floors and no ceilings in any of the rooms. The unfinished ceilings became a really serious problem at night when bats squeezed in between the tiles on the roof and came flying down throughout the house. We had brought our little dog, a toy poodle named Kidogo (African meaning *little one*), over with us. He could hardly wait until it was nighttime so he could join in our nightly batting practice. Sunny got on one side of the living room and I got on the other side. As the bats came flying down all around us, we swatted them down to the floor, and Kidogo attacked and killed them. Yea! Appropriately, Kidogo's other name was Killer.

Growing Pains from Within

This was about the only form of entertainment we had each night since we didn't have a TV or video player to watch. When we were not batting down the bats, we played various card and dice games to fill the balance of our evenings. Let me clear something up here—we had great devotion times at night as well, which came before any type of horseplay.

Let me tell you another very serious story concerning our dog Kidogo. One night I was up late preparing a message, and Kidogo kept dancing around my feet. I told him to go away, but he stayed there, dancing in and out by my feet. Finally, I looked and there was a small king cobra very close to my feet. Kidogo was bouncing in and out trying to keep the cobra away from my feet. I jumped up and did a size thirteen Mexican hat dance on the Cobra's head, killing him. Then I grabbed up Kidogo and gave him some much deserved loving to show him my appreciation for what he had done. Snakes are always a part of African life, whether in or out of town.

The church began growing quickly there, and soon overflowed our big living room. We went to two services, then three. God was quickly adding more servants to our stateside support team, as well as adding more funding to our monthly support, which had now tripled over our original support. We needed the new funds to keep up with our agreement on the house. We also needed those new funds to start looking for a permanent site where we could build a church building that could double as a classroom and build a large mission house there as well.

Our NGO required us to perform building projects in order to have an established mission base from which to work. This is not an easy step to complete with all the customary bribery delaying progress. God was ahead of us again and had placed a wonderful official named Ben Kalaba in our path, who was the assistant town clerk. A town clerk ranks higher than a mayor, so we had someone with power in office who was on our side.

He warned me that the land officer was a very corrupt individual and would be a big pain in the neck. Trying to get land through him quickly became an impossible thing for us, but not for our Lord. On three different occasions, this guy told us that our God had told him to issue us this one particular piece of land, then the very next day he pulled it back. It was the old reel you in and then cast you out thing. Ben told me to go over the heads of the local officials and bring in some top officials from the

Ugandan Investment Authorities, who were located at the capital. These people could come in and help put a stop to the land officer's game.

I did as Ben suggested and involved the Investment Authorities to gain the property acquisition. With the Investment Authorities' participation, I was able to present the facts. The land officer became furious and threatening, but I did not back down and requested the particular piece of property we had picked out be leased to us without any further delay. We explained that it was perfect for our needs and should be issued to us within three days because of all the previous unnecessary delays.

At the end of the meeting, Ben came up to me privately and gave me a very serious warning, "Jay, do not answer or go near your security gate at home at all for a couple of weeks as you have angered this man much, and here in Uganda, he might pay some thugs to come and kill you."

Wow! I said, "God did not bring me this far, Ben, for this man to be able to harm me. I'll be careful, but I won't lose any sleep over it." I still did not answer my security gate, and that was mostly at Sunny's wise request. Granted, some men we did not know came asking to see me twice and were told I was not available. Three days later we had our piece of land issued to us, with a yearly lease of only $75. Not bad for a one-and-a-half acre piece of land located in town.

Greg, Robert, and I got busy looking for a road grader to blade off tons of old broken sidewalks that were placed there after the city cleanup after all the wars. When they started cleaning it off, we had to get busy killing all the king cobras that had been living there under the debris—close to twenty of them. Most of them were still small, but some were six feet or longer.

When that was taken care of, we began planting thorn bushes as one of our protective barriers around the site. This was not an easy thing since we did not have any water on the site yet. We took our little van loaded with plastic Jeri cans to Lake Victoria a few blocks away, paid some local boys to fill them for us, and hauled the water back. Each of us took a Jeri can and watered the plants. We did this three times a week for two months until we were sure the young plants could make it on their own.

We had hired a young couple named Mike and Mary, and they had been working with us since the first house. Mike took care of the new property, and Mary worked with Sunny in the house. This was another requirement of the NGO—you must hire at least two nationals to work in your ministry. Mike and Mary always had a hard time finding and keeping a place to live, so we built a temporary 8'x12' house on the new site for them to live in rent free. Mike then became our guard at the house and caretaker for the land. They were as happy as two ducks in a pond just to have their own place to live in and a steady income.

We also brought two young women/girls into our home. Irene was swollen from beatings by her step-mom when she came to our gate seeking safety. Juliet came as an orphan when her aunt killed her mother. They became just like daughters to us, and we helped provide them with higher educations of their choice. We love them very much and would like to share their photos below.

Irene on the left; Juliet and little Sunny Jean on the right

A team of twenty-one interns came from our home church to be with us for six weeks. They worked hard to see and participate in all the work we were now doing so they could feel a part of each of the outreaches.

Shortly after we had arrived in Uganda, a Baptist missionary named Paul asked me to come to the prisons with him one Sunday, so I accepted. I got hooked on the first Sunday because these men and women really needed the truth. Paul said he was not a preacher and he could see that I would be able to meet the prisoners' needs better than he could at this time. He asked me if I would take that ministry over on a full-time basis, and I did. It didn't take long, and the attendance grew by the tens each time I was there. There were three men's prisons and one women's prison.

Part of our visiting team outreach was to go into the prisons. The men went with me, and the women went with Sunny. The team was really excited and wanted to bless these men with some great American worship, so I agreed and everyone was blessed. I then asked the team to sit down and let the prison worship group bless them. The prisoners cut loose on their drums and other types of African instruments, and the team went totally bananas. These men could really worship, and it left a lasting impression on the American visitors. I don't think there was a dry eye in the room, including mine, because the worship was so great.

Two people, named Jesse and Beverly, were a part of the team that day, and when we got home from the prisons they asked to talk to us. The first thing they told us was that they had been preparing to go to a South American country. Now, however, they felt God was telling them both to come and serve in the prisons and this was where they believed God wanted them to serve. They said they were from a very small church in Colorado and they could not see how they could raise enough support to come to Uganda. We told them that they never would be the ones to raise the needed support, that it was God's job, not theirs. If He gave them this calling, He would also provide for it in every way needed. We all prayed and came to believe God was calling them to Jinja.

Each week after they got back home, we heard from them, "You won't believe what's been happening; God is supplying from all over the place." We just answered back, "We told you so." Not really—we rejoiced with them at God's confirmation and blessings.

We also made sure the team got to see and enjoy points of interest in and near Uganda. We took them to Queen Elizabeth Game Park near Rwanda, located just inside some of the rebel-held territory. When we arrived at the park, there were about a hundred elephants grazing in the valley just below the lodge, and everyone went wild as cameras came flying out and film began clicking away.

Later, we all went to eat at a small local traditional restaurant nearby, and some hippos were feeding about a hundred feet away from the front door. Two of the men walked out very close to one of the hippos and began video taping. Suddenly, the hippo had enough of this and came charging. All you can see on one of the videos is sky then ground, sky then ground, because he was booking it for all he was worth. The men made it back to safety, but everyone became a little more respectful of the African wildlife after that.

That night, all the elephants came up into the lodge area and began feeding on the bushes and trees. To my surprise, many of the team had slipped outside to try to take some pictures in the dark. They had walked about a half a block away from their sleeping quarters, talking and giggling at what they were doing. Then one big old bull got tired of their flashes going off in his eyes and bolted toward them. If you have ever seen the Wylie Coyote and the roadrunner cartoon, that is what I got to see. Nothing but a dust cloud since all of them were yelling beep-beep and zooming down the road to safety. They all made it back to their rooms okay, but they had quite a story to tell when they got home. The rest of the night consisted of putting up with the noise of hippos, elephants, and rhinos grazing outside our windows.

We got up early to see if we could find any lions. We were told they were only a short distance outside the game park, so we went looking in our rented minibus. It had rained all that night, and our driver had never driven his bus off-road before. We got stuck deep in lion territory. Everyone had to get out and stay huddled close together, trying to look as big as possible to help confuse a lion should one come near. I had plenty of off-road experience, so I took the wheel and finally got it unstuck and turned around. Everyone quickly loaded back in, and I drove us, bouncing all the way, back to the highway. No one got to see any lions that day.

When we got back to the highway, I handed the driving duties back to our driver. We then went down the road away from the lodge, observing a large herd of antelope and warthogs going away from the game park, and—you guessed it—right toward rebel territory. We were about five miles down the road when we realized we had gone a little too far into rebel territory. This became apparent when we saw three vehicles about a half mile down the road in front of us being attacked and set on fire by rebels. More than likely, all the people were killed. Needless to say, we did a quick turnaround and booked it back toward the game park and safety.

The other outing we took them on was a rafting trip on the Nile River. This was a blast for everyone, as the whitewater rapids are classified as a category four trip. To give you some perspective, category five rapids are the most intense rapids you can go on anywhere in the world. Everyone had a great time, and we ended the day with a picnic, sodas, and a devotion time. Shortly after that, the team had to leave. Some of them headed to another outreach in Europe, and the rest went back home to the states.

Not long after that, the excitement of the team having been there began dying off, that we noticed a sudden change in Rose and Robert's attitude. They began being very secretive and short-tempered with us. They had never treated us like this before, and it was very hurtful to Sunny and me since we had always treated them like family—so much so that we all lived in the same house together. Robert began holding meetings with church members without my knowledge and without giving a reason. Whenever I asked anything, he got very angry and said I was not letting him run things. I reminded him that he was just in training and not really qualified to run things on his own at this time. The problem increased over the next few weeks.

One day, as Sunny was out shopping, I got a phone call from the police department telling me I was under arrest and needed to come to the police station immediately. I told them I would come as soon as my wife got back with the van. They got very hot with me and demanded I come right then. Again, I told them I would come as soon as I could get there.

I called my missionary friend, Paul, who was a very seasoned missionary and could advise me what to do. He came right over, and as soon as Sunny got home, he and I went to the police station. Robert had gone there and told them I was working with the rebels because I had some two-way radios in my container and said I was holding meetings with them regularly. Yes, I had two of these types of radios that had been donated, still in unopened boxes in my own private, locked trunks. It did not take a genius to figure out that Robert had been breaking into our belongings.

Paul took things over, talked privately with the officers and got them to let us settle this at home since he guaranteed them I was not working with the rebels in any way.

Back at home, Sunny and I became very concerned about having to live with this danger in our own home. Five days later, Robert did the same thing with another trumped-up charge. This time, I could prove him wrong quite quickly, and this made him even angrier with me. I noticed my trans-oceanic radio was missing, as well as my portable sound speaking system for village use.

I went to Robert and Rose's side of the house and knocked on their door. When Robert opened the door, I asked him for my two radios back, but he said he wasn't ready to return them right then. I told him if he didn't give them to me, I would go to the police to have him arrested for having stolen my property. He finally gave me the radio but not the speaker system.

About twenty minutes later, I heard my little motor bike going out of the compound. I looked at Sunny, Sunny looked at me, and we both knew he was going to the police station to place yet another false charge against me.

I got in the van and drove to the police station. I came in the door behind him while he was standing in front of two slightly drunk police officers and crying and yelling, saying, "That Muzungu (white person) I am living with just broke into my side of the house and threatened to kill me, my wife, and my children if I didn't give him all my belongings."

The police officer then asked him, "Is this man behind you that crazy man?"

Robert turned and looked, then began screaming, "Protect me, don't let him kill me."

Sad to say, the police officers were a bit drunk like I said earlier and told him to go home and that they were going to throw me in the cells for the night. In Uganda, you are guilty until proven innocent. You can imagine how busy I was praying by now, seeking God's help.

The officers came and grabbed me, shoving me around as much as two drunks could, saying, "You're going into the cells."

At this, I said a quick prayer to the Lord, "God, you say in your Word that when we are under trial, you will speak for us" (Matt. 10:19, paraphrase). Those words barely got out of my mouth when my hand flew out in front of me, and for about six or seven minutes I do not know what came out of my mouth toward these wide-eyed police officers. All I can tell you is that when the words stopped, the officers looked at me and said, "Pastor, you can go home now."

I did not say another word. I just took off for home and praised God all the way there. Robert and Rose could not believe their eyes when I came in and went to our side of the house where Sunny was waiting for me.

The next day, Sunny and I had had enough of this dangerous action from Robert and Rose, and we met with the officer in charge of all civilian disputes. We explained the danger we believed we were in and that we could not find a way to remove them.

He then called for Rose and Robert to come to his office immediately. While he was talking to all of us, Rose spoke up and said Robert was never ever a threat or danger to anyone. At this, Sunny remembered a story Rose told her and got up and said, "Let me tell you a story Rose recently told me about Robert."

This is what he did pertaining to his brothers when his father had died. Robert wanted all the land and the belongings, so he came up with the idea that he would take some poison and claim his brothers gave it to him to try and kill him. He would be able to have them arrested, and he could have everything. But he took a little too much poison and almost died.

At this, the officer listening told Rose and Robert they could leave but to stay away from the house until further notice and he would talk to them later. When they had left, he assigned three officers to come to our house and remove their belongings, placing them on the front porch. Everything would be inventoried and signed for that was placed on the porch. If anything belonged to us, we were to take it and record what it was. This we did, and we found numerous items from our container that Robert had taken and placed under his bed. He had been sending our items to his home village whenever we were away.

When Robert and Rose finally got to come home and found out they had been essentially evicted from the house, the sparks really flew. It was to no avail since the police officers stayed right there and controlled everything. They even tried to claim I stole money from their belongings when I supposedly threw their belongings outside. The officer quickly told them that it was he who had removed their items, he had two other officers as witnesses, and the charges they were making would be against him, not me. They quickly backed down and said no more.

Three days later, we were finally rid of them, but our hearts were broken. They were like our own children and their kids like our grandchildren. Pain can come from where you least expect it, and we have had more than our share over the years. It never gets easier, especially when it comes from other Christians. So much for loving one another. We bounced back, and everything kept growing. The house on the site was now finished, and our lease on the house on Labogo Road was coming to an end.

Chapter 9

Our Own Place at Last

I'VE HEARD IT said that prayer is the answer when you are in need of anything you cannot get done on your own. This is what most people end up doing, instead of letting God be in charge from beginning to end. We had to wait close to five years to get the site we were now moving into, and it took daily prayer to finally see it realized.

I can remember Sunny asking, "Honey, why are we not any further ahead than we are now? Are we going too slowly?" Her question stemmed from her seeing the other missions that had been out there for many years and had gotten where they were by doing just what we were doing, waiting on the Lord's perfect timing. Sure, I would have loved to have had some rapid growth, but that would have created a problem as to where I would have gotten the trained staff that it takes to meet the needs of such growth.

Remember that I told you how hard it was to get through the bureaucratic red tape in order to get our NGO license so we could register the mission. These same kind of delays are involved in almost everything you have to do in a third world country. Actually, we were not going slowly at all, and we had more people attending our church services than many of the churches that had been there three times as long. We just kept working on our God-given vision until it came to pass. You might feel a different kind of anxiety when you hit those big numbers and cannot find enough time or staff to take care of all that is required. This observation comes from my own experience from our rapid growth; it exploded after our final move, and we had very few staff members to help us.

The Making of a Missionary

The move to our site on Bell Avenue was a thrill for us. The team that had been out earlier helped us finish the church and get the new house we were building ready as well. After they left, Grace, our carpenter, Luke, our mason, and I worked from daylight until dark almost every day. I did not know very much about building, but by investigating other nearby projects and seeking advice wherever I could find it, we were getting the job done.

Grace was such a blessing to me because he could outwork five men and never slowed down. I owe him more than I could ever repay for his dedication, his heart, and the love he showed his Lord and us. He went on to help build many churches and other buildings for us. After Robert and Rose broke my heart, God knew I needed someone to take their places to ease my pain, so He gave me Grace and Luke.

What a thrill it was to see Sunny walking through the house, finally having a place to call home. Every woman needs to feel the security of having her own house, especially in such a struggling and unstable country as Uganda. I enjoyed watching and hearing her plan, "This goes here, that over there, and we'll need this or that." She was having a blast, and I was happy to be a part of her joy.

Julie N., our Interpreter, and Women's ministry asst

By now, the bushes we had planted were about six feet tall with long thorns on them. We could not afford chain link fencing all around the site yet, so the thorn bushes would have to do for now. I guess they would just have to poke the thugs a good one if they came around to try to rob us. We did have a fence around the house to secure the dogs and to keep any thugs at bay.

Some of the prisoners we had been training for six years were about to get out, and I could use some of them. One nice thing about training someone in prison is that he or she has plenty of time to study and seek the Lord.

I started using writing tablets for them while they were still in prison to write their Bible questions on, and I picked them up every Sunday and left the one from the week before. During the week, I answered their questions like mini-sermons. This method proved to be an excellent way to answer the questions since I did not have time to answer many on Sundays after the message.

Many of the prisoners grew to be godly men and began reaching out to other prisoners for Christ on their own. They began teaching the "through the Bible" studies three times a week. Paul, our main worker in prison, who was an ex-prisoner himself, helped make that ministry a success and was one of the first ones to come out of prison whom we put to work with the mission. We had tested others but discovered that they had quickly slipped back into their old worldly ways. Paul, though, began helping in the village ministries and with the church in Jinja. When he completed the required time out of prison for the prison officials to allow him to come back and minister at prisons, he began helping me there. Eventually, he began handling it all on his own. He also did most of my interpreting, especially when I needed to go to a village and share.

Stephan, another young man who had been attending our church services from the beginning, had grown strong in the faith as well. He approached me about moving back up to the northern area of Uganda to start a Bible study. He was from a village called Ogongora, which was in or near rebel-held territory. I began to fine-tune him for the work, as we sought the Lord in prayer about his request.

Meanwhile, we had received a message from Jesse and Beverly, the couple who felt called to come back and join the work in Jinja. They now had their support funding together and were ready to join us. It was such a blessing the day they arrived, as we watched them come down the ramp from the plane. Sunny and I both had tears of joy because we finally had someone from the states to share in the work with us. They both jumped into the workload as if they had been there for months.

Beverly and Sunny both went to the women's prison and Jesse and I went to the men's prison. After about six months, we could see that Jesse and Beverly were the ones to take those ministries over. They fine-tuned the ministries in ways I had never thought of and they grew even more. They found ways to provide medicines, seeds for crops, clothing, and transport to and from the hospital when people were sick. This might not sound like much unless you knew how much these prisoners had to suffer. The prisoners ate only ground cornflower called maize twice a day, and there were few medicines, which the guards quickly stole and sold to the clinics in town. Beverly was quite a schemer about how to get around all these hindrances. When Beverly and Jesse finally got all their plans in place, the prisoners were being properly fed and were receiving better health care—not what you and I would accept, but better.

The Calvary Chapel Bible study we had started in Iguluibi had now grown to a size that meant we needed to build a permanent church building for it. Many of you have never experienced a real miracle, and neither had Jessie. Jesse had only been in Jinja about a month when we headed out to the village in the van to start building. The night before it had rained heavily, and the village roads were almost impassable. Still, we loaded all our supplies and headed out. Shortly after we got to our turnoff, we could see it was going to be very rough going.

When we were about two thirds of the way, we came to what looked like a small lake located between some tall sugarcane. We got out and checked it out and decided that since we had come this far, we ought to try to make it the rest of the way. I looked for all the high spots to try to ride on, prayed for the Lord's help to get across, and then headed out.

A little over halfway across, we sunk down in the water up to our axels in some mud and were unable to move forward or backward. I looked at Jesse and said, "Jesse, the only way we are going to get out of this mess is for the Lord to send a multitude of people to push us out." KAZAM! Out of the bushes came people from everywhere; they hardly said a word, but they got around the van and pushed us out the other side to dry ground. I had just been to the bank and had a bunch of one thousand shillings notes, each worth about sixty cents. I got out and began giving each person one, and when I had finished with the last person, I was out of the shillings I had brought. God's plans are way ahead of ours. Never forget that, because He does things right down to the last penny (or shilling).

Beverly also took over our orphan program. We had about sixteen kids, some of whom were real orphans, some had AIDS, but all were in deep need of love and tender care. Beverly had the gifts to take good care of them. She became a tough but loving "Mama Beverly" to them all. Most of them lived next door in an abandoned building and lacked any discipline, so she came up with ways to get their attention. She also sent out prayer requests for supporters for each of them, and her prayers were answered. She ran a tight ship on those funds and the kids so neither could be abused.

When Sunny got too sick to go to the prisons anymore, she trained some of our girls from the church to help her. Some were already trained, but we needed many more. One of Bev's greatest blessings to the mission was that she had a pretty good knowledge of medicine and illnesses. She functioned as our doctor, house mom, and caretaker. She also undertook a very difficult ministry at a poor village nearby called "Local."

Local was an old railroad living quarters site, and people stayed in what looked like cattle stalls, most of them filthy. It also had more than its share of drunkards and people with drug problems. Bev was faithful, going every week and showing them that she loved them. No matter what any of them did to try to hinder that ministry, she still came, rain or shine.

Stephan was finally ready to go up north to work at his village. Jesse and Beverly had not been up that way yet, so we all loaded up Stephan's stuff and headed for Ogongora. When we got deep in the bush where his mother lived, we found out that her mud house had burned down a couple of nights before. So the meeting there was both joyous and sad. We gave Stephan some funds with which to help his mother and to help him get started with the ministry back in the village.

Jesse began a School of Ministry (SOM) in the church building after they had settled in a bit. The SOM has become a wonderful way of training and maturing the growth of those we could see God calling into ministry. Teaching was a special anointing God had given Jesse and Beverly. Jesse ran all the school programs from start to finish, plus handling all of his prison ministries.

We were now having two church services and still growing. The church doubled in number of people attending. Jesse also filled in for me in the church whenever I had to go to the villages or at other times when I was away for any length of time.

Satan tried hard to close the prison ministry over the years, but God always won the battle in the end. The prison ministry also requires servants who do not discourage easily and can hang in there when the going gets tough. Jesse was the right man for the job then, and he still is.

Life on the mission field is not all work. At times we had to take breaks just to keep our sanity. Mission work can take a heavy toll on a person's health and mental state. You go full bore from early morning until late at night. We averaged about seventeen-hour days either studying, teaching, ministering to someone's needs, or dealing with some government issue. It never stops, from the time you arrive on the field until you leave years later.

Please don't get me wrong here—I'm not complaining. I'm just saying that you need to take a break at times to get some much-needed and well-earned rest so you don't burn out. You will hit peaks and valleys in any type of work, but especially in mission work. When those low times hit, you will ask yourself, "Why do I keep doing this over and over?"

It is because God put it on your heart, and until He takes it away from your heart, you will stay—no matter what is happening or what the conditions are.

We had two main places where we liked to go to get away. The first was all the way in Mombasa on the Kenyan coastline. For forty dollars a night, you got a very nice room and all-you-can-eat supper and breakfast. They had plenty of excellent entertainment, and you could go swimming in the Indian Ocean or just lie under the palm trees sucking on your favorite soda or juice.

The second place was also in Kenya at the Lake Nakuru National Park. The park has just about every type of wild game you could hope to see, great food, and plush living quarters—a bit more expensive than the beach but very well worth it. Nakuru was also much quicker for us to reach. We have awesome pictures of lions right up in our faces at the door of our truck. Rhinos came as close as twenty feet away, as did warthogs, gazelles, antelope, panthers, leopards, giraffes, monkeys, and even some snakes. The best thing about this leisure time was that we were unloading all the weight we had been carrying and having some fun for a change. Afterwards, of course, it was back to Jinja and to all our loving work.

About a year later, Stephen came and said he needed me to come and see the work God was doing through him. So we took off in the truck that our home church, Calvary Chapel Albuquerque, had just bought us and headed for Soroti, our jumping-off point to go on to his village in Ogongora. We arrived deep in the village near where his mother lived, close to twenty miles into rebel-held territory. The place was in deep drought with little water anywhere and no crops growing in the fields. The people were nearing starvation, not just for the Word, but also for physical nourishment.

Stephen gave me some shocking news about how many of the children were dying. He told me that three out of five babies were dying from either malnutrition, diarrhea from the bad water, or deadly malaria, not to mention AIDS. Other people were also dying because they could not get to medical help quickly enough. They had to wait near one of the village roads and hope that an old van being used as a taxi would come by with any room on it. Sadly, most of them died sitting alongside the road waiting.

When we went back to town, I loaded up with food and some medicines, using the funds I had brought with me as far as they would go. We returned to the village and began distributing it. We gave first to the most needy and then meted out the balance to those who were left.

When I got back to Jinja, I could not get the thought of all those babies dying off my mind. I put out a prayer request with the cost figures to build a small but expandable clinic and to put in a public well in that village.

God works fast if we are caring for others more than ourselves. It wasn't long until the funds began coming in. We bought some of the materials and went and worked until they were finished. This kept up for months, but the work paid off. We now had a two-building eight-room clinic where the people could get medical help. But we still needed to get a qualified staff and supplies and get the paperwork done to get the well put in. I knew the well would take at least a month since there was a waiting list ahead of us.

Pastor Stephen Okello, Ogongora Calvary Chapel

Earlier at the same site we had received enough funds to finish Stephen's church building, which has a new addition since then. Stephen still takes care of his flock both spiritually and physically. He has never asked anything for himself. He is truly a godly man.

We were having some growing pains and needed to get serious about adding a new two-story structure on our site. Jesse and Beverly had been living in the house with us since they had arrived, and it was time to set them up with some space of their own. Some of our other staff members were having a hard time finding a place to live. So we went back to prayer, sharing our need for another building project. The Lord got right to work and the funds came rolling in. I am not a contractor, yet with the Lord's help and by asking questions of those who had the know-how, we got the work going.

Chapter 10

Baptizing Can Be Dangerous

I N THE CHAPTER about our first mission trip to Mbale, Uganda, I described many of the dangerous times we experienced, but I didn't include a story about three young men from another mission group whom we were told about shortly after we arrived on our first calling.

The three, ranging in age from their late teens to early twenties, were told not to go swimming in a nearby stagnant, disease-infested stream. They paid no attention to this advice and headed out, thinking they had nothing to worry about. They spent an hour or two swimming and then returned to their mission base.

By nighttime they all were very sick. By the next morning, one of the young men was so deathly ill that he was not responding to any of the medicine. By late that same afternoon, he collapsed into a coma and died in his parents' arms. The next day, the second young man got worse, and within just a few short hours he was gone as well. His parents, like the others, were totally devastated. The third young man seemed to be doing well for about a week, then slowly lost the battle and died.

The source of the deadly micro-organisms that killed them was the many decaying bodies that floated in the rivers and lakes for extended periods of time because of all the wars in Uganda. These organisms became a thriving, strong bunch of death, just waiting for their victims. When you are serving on a foreign mission field and someone advises you not to do something, understand that they know what they are talking about. At the very least, you should check it out with others before you leap into something that might bring you to your last dying breath.

Pastor Jay Baptizing Irene

We performed baptisms regularly in the rivers near Mbale, but we made sure that the water was swift enough to keep the micro-organisms from being able to breed. Such organisms are more numerous and dangerous when in standing water, which also allows mosquitoes to reproduce. The river we went to was safe, and we never had anyone get any kind of sickness from going in the water there. I had asked many other missionaries where the best place was to baptize safely, and they were the ones who advised me to use the place we used.

God tells us in Proverbs 8:32-36 that "hearing instruction leading unto God finds life, those that hate God love death." Then Proverbs 11:14 tells us, "In the multitude of counselors there is safety." But let me add this one from 19:20, "Listen to counsel and receive instruction, that you may be wise in your latter days" (paraphrase).

In Proverbs 15:22 God tells us, "Without counsel, plans go awry, but in the multitude of counselors they are established." Only a fool does not listen to wisdom; do not be a fool, be safe.

When we came to Jinja, which is located at the source of the Nile River, the water is fast, clean, and plentiful. Where could any danger be lurking in such a beautiful setting? I was asked by one of our village pastors named Paul to come and perform a baptism service in his village with him. He had quite a few members who wished to be baptized. So I rented a twenty-one-passenger mini-van to carry everyone to a nearby location we could use for baptism.

As with anything we did in the village, many wanted to come just to view everything we did. We drove to our secluded spot on the Nile River. It had a cove branching off from the main river that would be just slow enough so we could go into the water safely. Eighteen people waded out to me to be baptized.

I took about twenty minutes to explain what baptism is all about and another fifteen minutes to perform the actual baptismal service. Everyone was excited, and most of them were very frightened at being dunked beneath the water for the first time in their lives. Most feared dying while under the water, but their excitement overrode their fear. We finished the service with prayer, and everyone came out of the water.

The whole time we were in the water a man had been standing a short distance away, watching us with great concern on his face. So I walked over to greet him and ask him why. He smiled a beautiful smile and then said, "Did you know that there are three crocodiles right over there by those bushes?"

This definitely got my attention, and I snapped my head in the direction of the crocodiles he was pointing at. Sure enough, there were three very large crocodiles sunbathing and looking straight at us. I asked him why he had not told us about them earlier. He stated that by this time of day, they are finished hunting and just want to rest. But, he said, if they had moved to come our way, he would have yelled at us to get out of the water quickly. So much for blind ignorance and diving headlong into a situation that could have brought harm to many of us! We counted our blessings and went back to Paul's church and then home.

The Calvary Chapel in Iguluibi called and asked Jesse and me to come do a baptism service near their village, so Jesse and I headed out to do our thing. Some of the people had walked down to the site in Lake Victoria and we drove the rest there in our truck. Altogether, twenty-seven people were seeking baptism.

Again, we went out into the water and began explaining what we were about to do. Many other villagers watched from the bank. The whole process took about an hour and a half to finish. Like the other time, there were some men standing nearby, whom we had noticed looking off in one particular direction quite often.

Jesse and I walked over to them and asked if we could ask them some questions. "Sure," they said, and continued looking often to the same place we had seen them looking earlier. We finally asked, "Why do you keep looking over in that direction?" We had looked over there and had seen nothing. We knew they were fishermen and knew Lake Victoria well since they fished it every day.

They told us that some crocodiles were swimming over by that palm tree. The tree was about a hundred yards away, and we still could not see anything. Then, lo and behold, four crocodiles surfaced around the same time and began splashing around, eating something they had just caught. We stood with our mouths wide open in shock, but we were glad they were not having us for lunch.

In the past, few crocodiles inhabited Lake Victoria or the Nile River until the crisis that occurred in Rwanda between the Hutus and the Tutsis. Three hundred and fifty thousand people were needlessly massacred in just a few days, and this became one of the worst bloodbaths in recent history. Many of those bodies floated down the rivers into Lake Victoria, then on into the rivers that stemmed from it. With many of the dead bodies now floating in the river and moving away from their natural habitat, the crocodiles just kept eating and following the dead bodies right into Lake Victoria.

Here we were in our ignorance again, out baptizing in crocodile-infested water up to our waists. Dumb, dumb, and then really dumb. Thank You, Lord, for watching over dummies like us.

We also held other baptism services that presented no danger to anyone. Like I said, most village people are afraid of going under water, and I had a hard time hanging onto them when they first started under. Legs and arms started flying everywhere as I pushed them down deep into the water, giving them what they came for, a drowning—just kidding.

The fun started when they came out of the water, screaming and waving their arms, yelling, "Alleluia, alleluia, praise the Lord, alleluia!" I am not sure if they were yelling because they had just been baptized or because I did not drown them. Nevertheless, they loved every second of it—that is, after it was all over and they were on dry land again.

Chapter 11

Some Near Death Experiences

STAYING HEALTHY ON the mission field is always a big concern. You cannot easily get health insurance to cover you on the mission field, especially if you are in a third world country. In Europe or some other developed country it might be possible. But even if you can find a company that will issue you a policy for a third world country, you could probably not afford it. The ones I heard about were more than half of that person's support for each month. That would usually be over $750 a month because of the high risk areas we mostly worked in.

A man who was associated with us for a while told me it was no different for us on the field than for those at home because we all suffer. Let me share with you the scenario I gave him.

What happens when you are in a car accident out in the country in the states and it is serious and people are badly hurt? First, phones are available nearby, or someone can go and call for help. Then you can get police help, an ambulance, even an air-ambulance if necessary. They take you to a modern hospital, which has highly-trained doctors and is very sanitary. You have a nice clean room to stay in while you recover.

Let's examine the same scenario in a third world country. Most likely you will lie beside the road and die while onlookers steal all your belongings, like your wallet and anything else they can grab. If, by some miracle, a good Samaritan should happen to stop and help you, what can he do? He cannot call for an ambulance because there isn't one. There is c no helicopter. Maybe they can put you in the back of a pickup t.

you might be laid on a dirty seat. Most people will not touch you at all if you are bleeding, because of their fear of getting AIDS.

If this good Samaritan takes you to get help, where does he take you? Maybe it's to a hospital that smells of old urine, with broken windows and filth everywhere you look and mosquitoes and flies buzzing around. Next, the poorly-trained staff tries to treat you with their haphazard equipment. Some places are a little better than others, but most likely you are going to get very poor to terrible treatment in most non-developed countries.

The man who spoke with me was partly right—we all do suffer everywhere, but definitely not in the same way, by any means. We may all live in houses, but even they are not the same. A mud hut is a mud hut, and a brick house is still a brick house. I think you get the picture. The circumstances make it totally different.

Sunny was able to find an American-trained female Ugandan doctor named Grace. She even had some of her staff sent to America for advanced training. This type of health care has only become available in the last few years. Thank God we had our Dr. Grace to look after Sunny's medical issues. Sunny had a serious yeast problem like so many other women get, but hers had accelerated out of control, and it was quickly taking Sunny's health away.

In reality, Sunny was dying right before our eyes and we didn't really know it. She spent many hours searching the Web, trying to find an answer for getting rid of the yeast infection, but she got little help. We made a decision to head home to find a specialist in the field of yeast infections.

The first time home, we didn't accomplish much in the way of finding help for her. Mainly, they just offered new types of diets that did very little in the way of help. Things would not be any better if she stayed home, so we went back to Uganda. Sunny kept her search up until one day she read something on the Web from a lady who said that her yeast infection was stemming mostly from the mercury fillings in her mouth. Mercury, as we found out, is an accelerator for rapid yeast growth in the body. Mercury is what amalgam fillings are mostly made up of, yet the dental industry claims strongly that they cannot hurt you. This might be true if you only have one or two fillings in your mouth. Sunny had ten. You be the judge of the following information.

Back on furlough we went. This time we searched out a doctor who knew how to handle her mercury poisoning. We found a specialist who dealt with this every day, and he did a mercury count on Sunny. Listen carefully: a person is only allowed a three count of mercury in his or her system, but because Sunny had ten mercury-filled teeth in her mouth, the count came back a twenty-four count. Sunny should have been dead from that much mercury in her system since this was eight times the allowable limit. She was slowly dying of mercury poisoning, and the doctor told her to get a dentist to remove the fillings as soon as possible. He also said she might want the mercury replaced with porcelain fillings.

We found out afterwards, however, that this is a very dangerous thing to have done. If the dentist doesn't protect you properly from breathing in the mercury vapors or dust from the drill, you can actually overdose and possibly die during the drilling procedure. We made the mistake of price shopping the cost of it because we did not have much money to work with. We used a shopping mall dentist who seemed straight out of dental school and did not use any type of protection on Sunny.

Consequently, all the vapors and dust went straight into her system. After the dental work was finished, Sunny's health took a nosedive. We rushed back to the specialist, and he did another mercury count on her—it was one hundred and fifty. In all actuality, Sunny should have been dead. They worked as fast as possible, which was three times a week in flushing this extra mercury out of her system. As soon as the levels started down toward the normal side, her health began to improve. By the end of the second month, her health was better than it had been in over ten years. That's a long time to suffer from something an industry says won't hurt you.

Today, Sunny still fights a small yeast infection at times, but it does not harm her like it did when it was stealing her health away. Here is the big difference in her health: before, she was so weak that I had to wheel her around in a wheelchair, but when we went back to Uganda, she outran me everywhere we went—with a big smile on her face.

Thank you, Lord, for having your hands on my Sunny's life, and for saving her from certain death.

There have been many changes on the African mission field in the last few years, but things are still way behind a developed area like Europe or America. You can find a decent dentist or doctor if you look hard enough and ask enough questions. It will mainly depend on where you are serving, so please investigate before you go there. You must have knowledge ahead of time as to what is available so you will know what to expect. It is far better to be somewhat prepared than to go out blindly and be caught at a loss as to what to do in an emergency and end up suffering needlessly.

The mercury poisoning wasn't our only brush with death. Early one Sunday morning, as I headed to do my ministry at the prison, I had just driven the van through the first security gate and was about a block down the road. Suddenly, shots started whizzing past my windows. I could not see clearly where they were coming from because it was raining so heavily. I stopped and saw some of the guards running around looking for some escaped prisoners. They were shooting wildly out over the brush area, which was near where I had stopped. I never saw a prisoner, though.

The guards ran to where I was and jumped into my van, telling me to back up and quickly go around to the other side of the brushy area. I did as they asked and headed for the other side. As I went, I began to think—if they caught these guys and they saw me helping the guards, I would be at risk when I went into the main body of prisoners to do church services. For that reason, when I got close to where they needed me to take them, I stopped. The guard sitting right behind me placed his gun against my head and said that if I did not go on up, he would shoot me right then. I grabbed the barrel of his gun and shoved it down into the seat, telling him to get out. At this, the other guards jerked him out and said, "Leave the pastor alone, as he has already helped enough."

The next morning, I went to see the warden of the prison and explained what the guard had done in the excitement of pursuit. He became furious at the man's placing my life in danger or threatening my life for any reason. He removed the guard from all duties, and I did not see him there anymore.

Another near-death experience occurred when I got a very rare strain of malaria. It was some kind of Asian malaria, and none of the medicines we had would even begin to work on it. Malaria attacks mostly the valves of your heart, and you get severe chills like a severe case of the flu. I was shaking so badly that Sunny was lying on top of me trying to keep me from bouncing off the bed. My heart was banging up and down in my chest as it tried to pump the blood through my body. I was sure that I was not going to make it this time, especially after three days of getting seriously worse.

One of the missionaries told Sunny to take me over to where the Chinese doctors were staying because they had some herbal malaria medicine from China that might work. They all loaded me up, and off we went across town to the Chinese team. They gave me a triple dose of the medicine, and within four hours I began to feel it working. I began to breathe a sigh of relief, just at the fact I was still able to breathe. By the end of the week, I was ready to go back to work.

Another close call came from a recluse spider bite. This bite is very dangerous because you can get a serious infection from it. The toxin from the spider's bite starts eating away the flesh, dissolves it, and does not stop easily. We again had tried almost every antibiotic in town, but gangrene set in, and it started racing throughout my leg. Needless to say, I was afraid I was going to lose my leg because it was looking so terrible and swollen twice the normal size.

Again, a missionary who had just recently arrived from England had brought a new strong type of triple-antibiotic. They gave me a heavy shot right away, and we saw some of the redness leave within about thirty minutes. After a couple of days, and two more shots, the redness was almost gone. We all breathed a sigh of relief. I felt like getting up and doing a jig on my leg, just to thank the Lord for the medicine. Later on, I was bitten a second time, but that time I knew what to do and where to get the right medicine.

I do not know for sure if I was in any real danger in this next situation, but it was very scary nonetheless. I needed to get up early to head for Kampala to do some business there. As I walked toward the taxi park, I came upon a pack of wild dogs. There were about twenty of them, and they definitely looked hungry. They started circling around and were getting too close for comfort. I do not know what made me do what I did next, but I growled very loudly and ran straight for what I thought was their leader. The funny thing is, it worked, and they took off running in one direction, and I in the other. I laughed all the rest of the way to catch my taxi.

During all these experiences, we had a multitude of people praying for us at home and in Africa. God heard and answered all those prayers— praise, glory, and thanks to our heavenly Father.

Chapter 12

Street Kids Can Be Dangerous

WHEN THE VAN we were buying came into the port in Mombasa, I was told I would have to travel there to clear it through customs at the port. The dealer I bought it from had told me he had already taken care of everything. So much for trusting a third world wheeler-dealer! We prayed for my safety on the trip, and then I headed out for the border to catch an overnight train to Nairobi. I would arrive there about nine in the morning to catch the next train at six in the evening for Mombasa on the Indian Ocean coast.

When I arrived in Nairobi the next morning, I gathered up my belongings and headed out to find a place to spend the day. This sounds very innocent, but on the way toward one of the big hotels nearby, I came upon some rowdy street kids. They began trying to force me to give them money, but after having lived there once before, I had learned the hard way that it is not a good idea to give to these kids. If you do, they will not leave you alone and will follow you wherever you go.

I tried to gently avoid them, but they kept pushing in against me on all sides, trying by this time to pick my pockets. Finally, I raised my voice and told them very firmly in Swahili they needed to go away. Suddenly, I felt a sharp jab in my buttocks through my Levi's. I spun around and tried to grab the little turkey, but they took off running in every direction. I did not think much more about it and just went my way.

Later that day as I was reading the local newspaper, I came upon an article that sent chills and fear running up my spine. The ad stated that a missionary was waiting at a stoplight in his car with his window down when two street boys came up to him and began begging for money. He told them, as I had done, that he was not going to give them anything. One of the boys right next to him quickly jabbed him in the arm with a needle. He jumped out and chased the boy down, got the needle, and took it to the AIDS center to be tested. A few weeks later, his whole world changed drastically when the test came back showing that both the needle and his blood sample later tested positive for the AIDS virus.

When I got to the part that stated it was positive for AIDS, my heart sank to my feet. I literally could not even stand up because I had become so weak-kneed. I began crying out in prayer to the Lord for His merciful protection and cleansing power to be upon my life. Within moments, a real peace flowed over me to calm me, and the fear left. Then I started thinking about what I might need to do about it. I decided that I must go on as if nothing had happened, at least until I returned home, and not call Sunny and scare her. I thought it would be better if I was standing right next to her when I broke the news of what had happened.

I went by train to Mombasa where I was met by a young Muslim man who was a relative of the man from whom I had purchased the van. I was supposed to spend my five days there living in his apartment. This became a very serious test of my knowledge of Scripture. He was a very devout Muslim and began bringing sheiks from the Muslim mosque where he went for prayers four times a day. These sheiks brought propaganda videos trying to defeat my belief in God's Word and show me that the writers of the Bible had erred in their interpretation of different events and the people involved in those events.

I explained that the Koran was written over six hundred years after Christ had already ascended into heaven and long after Scripture had been completed. I continued to say that they were the ones who had to make it say whatever Mohammed wanted it to say. Well, needless to say, this did not go down well.

The next night, he brought a visiting senior sheik from Saudi Arabia, who did most of Islam's debating against the Bible. When I say my knowledge was put to the test, it was put to the test to the max. This guy was good at twisting my words and then playing on them.

Remember this: God says in Mark 13:11, "Whenever you are under trial, I will speak for you" (paraphrase). Therefore, I began praying that

God would use me as a vessel for Him to speak through to defeat this hotshot sheik. The main defense of a Muslim when he feels he is losing an argument is to start yelling at you to get you confused. God is not at all fearful of a false god since He is God. God gave me the strength to stand strong, and the verses He kept giving me frustrated this sheik to where they began throwing things around the apartment. I finally said that our conversation was over and just walked away and headed for my room. They kept arguing for a long time afterwards, and then all became quiet.

I asked my host not to bring any more of those types of people over because I wanted the chance to get to know him better and properly thank him for allowing me to stay there. I ended up getting him a good book on how to witness to a Muslim, and he promised to read it. I hope he read that and also the Bible I gave him.

A few days later, I crossed the border back into Uganda. I had hardly gotten into the house when Sunny ran and grabbed me and said, "Honey, what is wrong?" This shook me, as I had not said anything to anyone. Yet my wife could see that I was carrying a heavy burden on my heart. She said I looked fearful and downcast as I drove in the driveway. I told her that we needed to talk later about something that happened in Nairobi.

Sunny said, "Sorry, honey, not later; we are talking right now," and into the house we went. When we got into the bedroom, I laid out the whole story and waited for her response. Sunny immediately grabbed me and said, "Honey, nothing, but nothing changes between us—nothing." I told her that might be easy for her to say since she would not be the one who would cause her mate to suffer unto death, should I test positive for AIDS.

Things are not easy when you go to get tested for AIDS. My heart is more sympathetic now for those who are going through what I did. The initial test came back negative, and we received a small breath of fresh air. The next six weeks, during which you have to wait for the second and main test, seemed like a lifetime. We went and got my testing and were told we now had to wait another three weeks for the results to come back. Three weeks went by slower than the six, and we entered the office filled with serious anxieties racing over us. We were called back to a private room and went through another thirty minutes of waiting, which was now as if a lifetime had gone by. Finally, the doctor came in and wasted no time in giving us an answer. He stated that I had been found negative for the AIDS virus. We jumped up and shouted and cried a bunch because we were so relieved by the test results. We then went and had a nice celebration meal at a very nice restaurant. After that, we went home and crashed, because we were so exhausted from all the weeks of having to wait on results.

What possibly kept me from being infected by the needle was that it hit where my hip pocket was folded over. This caused the needle to be cleansed somewhat and a bit restricted from entering all the way into my behind. This sounds reasonable, but we are giving God the credit, not my Levi's.

Chapter 13

Some Village Experiences

CALVARY CHAPEL JINJA was growing rapidly, and so were the five other village churches we had planted. Two of them had ex-prisoners as their pastors. We did much of their training while they were still in prison; then Jesse fine-tuned them when they got out. They also had to go through a time of testing to make sure the world would not pull them back into their old ways. Some did not make it and slid back into trouble.

Another problem in Africa is hyperactive false teaching. Some false teachings claim that all our weaknesses are demons and need to be cast out. Scripture clearly teaches otherwise. "Greater is He Who is in you, than he who is in the world"(1 Jn 4:4, paraphrase). In addition, Christ is called the Light unto the world (Jn 1:9, paraphrase), so if He is the Light, how can darkness enter where there is light? Simply put, it cannot because Christ never ever leaves us or forsakes us.

Some of these groups also like to exalt the spiritual gifts. They claim that you are not a born again Christian if you do not speak in tongues or have some other special type of gift. I believe that all the gifts are there for us today. Acts 1:8 defines exactly how to know when you have received the Holy Spirit.

"But you shall receive **POWER** when the **HOLY SPIRIT** has come upon you; and you shall be **WITNESSES to Me** in Jerusalem, and in all Judea and Samaria, and to the **END of the EARTH.**"
—emphasis added

The Making of a Missionary

As a missionary in foreign lands, many times you will need an interpreter to make sure that what you are saying is fully understood and that you are not sounding like a crazy person. You can see from some of these examples what we went through in trying to reach people who have been deceived into believing they have a gift that makes them greater and have more power than any other Christian. We can understand how easily they are led astray—the witch doctor can get them to believe his lies of power because they fear that he will place some kind of spell on them.

Let me share a story with you about when we were invited to a traditional healer's convention. Most of these healers are into some form of witchcraft or are witch doctors themselves. I asked Jesse, and also Julie, who did much of my interpreting for me, to come and assist with our part of the program.

We went, and as I was about halfway through my message, two cars drove up very close to the structure where everyone was listening. The people in the cars got out and strolled slowly right in front of where I was speaking. I am not a person who will tolerate being shown such disrespect, and I asked them to hurry to their seats and please be quiet.

We found out within a few moments that the main woman in the group was the chief witch doctor of all Uganda. She did not remain quiet for long and began chanting and mumbling in a low voice. I stopped again and asked her to please be quiet. At that, the bodyguards she came with jumped up as if they were going to attack me. God put it on my heart to firmly tell them to sit down, which I did, and they sat right back down.

I tried to continue with the message, but within minutes she was at it again, and I stopped and started to address her, but little soft-spoken Julie stopped me and said she wanted to tell this woman in her language to be still because we had the power of God on our side. Julie went straight over to her table and placed her hands firmly down in front of the witch doctor and began letting her have it. When she was finished she came back over to me and said, "You can begin now, Papa Jay."

Just as I started, the woman jumped up and ran out to her car and began pounding on the hood of her car, crying and yelling, "He has taken away my power, he has taken away my power."

I turned to the other people there and stated that she did not have any power but what they had allowed her to have by falsely believing in her. I then told our host that we would wind up our portion and leave the rest to them. I finished, and as we started to pack to leave, the host and other members were all in a huddle, talking about what had just happened. They came hurrying over to us and said they did not want us to leave because everyone there wanted to know where they could get the same power we had that could defeat a witch doctor. At that, Jesse and I did some teaching on the gospel message of Christ.

Lumuli is another one of the villages just north of Jinja. Pastor Paul, who is an ex-prisoner and was third in command at our mission, was the pastor there for a while. Paul asked us to come up there and do a crusade. We had not done one before, so I agreed to come. He started making plans, and he went all over that village area sharing with the people about what was going to happen in his little church. We came with our little speaker system and our wonderful worship group and got it all set up.

We had been praying that many of the people in that area would actually show up, hear the message, and be saved. We started our worship with about forty visitors, more than those who usually attended services. Within twenty minutes, close to a hundred people had come, and more were coming down the roads and paths. This little church was not going to hold that many people, yet they just kept squeezing in. The ones who could not get inside began sticking their heads through the windows and door; the place was packed tighter than a sardine can.

The worship was fantastic, and the people were really enjoying feeling what it was to worship the Lord with all their heart, mind, and soul. Finally, it came time for me to give the message. The people were getting excited over the message, and when I made the altar call, over fifty people came forward to accept Christ as their personal Lord and Savior. We went home floating on cloud nine at God moving so strongly in that village and our seeing so many new souls for His kingdom and glory.

When you teach the truth, people are changed, as it is that truth that sets people free. Jesse also did some crusades and got the same results. It is not the pastor, but the Lord Who is at work in the listeners. You had better know the truth, or else not get up and proclaim that you do, because God will hold you accountable for each false word you feed to His children.

Another notable time was when Stephan asked me to come to Ogongora to show the *Jesus* film. I loaded up the projector and the videos, some sodas, and junk food, and headed north to Ogongora. While I was setting things up, Stephen came to me and said we had a big problem. He told me that two men were going around telling everyone that I was the antichrist. I had worn short pants to set up since it was very hot outside, and I have a tattoo of Mighty Mouse on my right calf from my Navy days.

I asked Stephen to have everyone come into the church, including the men who were telling the story. After everybody was in, I raised my leg onto a tabletop for everyone to see. I asked them to come up and see what I had on my leg. I also reminded them that they decorate their bodies with razor cuts in certain patterns, and that did not make them the antichrist.

I then opened my Bible and taught a quick message on how to recognize the mark of the anti-Christ and approximately when and where he would be seen. They actually got a kick out of me having a mouse on my leg. As for the two men, I addressed them privately and made sure they knew to be more careful about jumping to conclusions and causing such a problem. But I also told them I was glad to see that they were trying to protect the body of Christ from the enemy.

Luke, our mason on left, Grace our builder on right,
and the clinic at Ogongora Calvary Chapel

When I showed the *Jesus* film that night, we had over two hundred people who had walked from as far as thirty miles away. You see, most of the villagers had never seen a movie or a video, and they believed everything they saw on the screen to be actually happening right in front of them. They wailed, cried, and wailed some more. When the night was finished, more than eighty people came to know Christ as their Lord and Savior. The only downside was that there were millions of mosquitoes eating us all alive. Yes, you guessed it—I got a pretty bad case of malaria, but it was worth it.

Kajansi was our newest village church, and one of our best pastors from prisons, Cosmos, headed it. We had just picked up another team from the states at the airport and were taking them to a crusade at this church to let them see life in the village.

This time, things did not go as well because people seemed more interested in the food that was being prepared behind the building than in listening to the gospel message. Even Cosmos and some of my own staff were more interested in checking on the food and socializing than in making sure people were getting spiritually fed. Because of this, I cut the message short and wrapped things up. God says not to cast your pearls before swine, and when people treat His Word like they were doing, they fit the category.

Chapter 14

Tanks for the Dust

TOWARD THE END of our work in Uganda, a high-level government official called me concerning 18,000 refugees seeking shelter, food, and water. These refugees were deep inside a highly-active rebel territory in the northern area near Sudan. The official said she had tried other missions and agencies, but no one wanted to go into such a dangerous area. Someone had told her that I already had built a clinic not far from where these refugees were gathering for protection from a small army detachment located there. She asked if I would go there to try to meet the needs of the people since so many had died.

Some had died from the rebel snipers shooting at them when they sneaked outside the camp in an attempt to find food or water. Others were dying from the lack of proper food, water, or medical attention. I asked the official if she could get me flown into the camp by one of their army helicopters. She quickly agreed to my request. She even gave me some officers' names and phone numbers, whom I could count on to provide us with the protection we would need going into the camp and back out to safety.

I began by e-mailing all our supporters and our home church, giving them all the details and possible cost figures and asking for everyone to pray and seek God's will upon these devastated peoples' lives. Grace (our carpenter), Stephen (our pastor in that area of the country), and I met together in Soroti at the office of the general who would be flying us in and out of the camp in his assigned chopper. I had also contacted Samaritan's

Purse, an organization that also deals with refugee camps, to go with me and help find the best plan of action for the problem facing us.

We all loaded onto the chopper and headed for our destination. I could not help but laugh at Grace and Stephen. Neither man had ever been near anything like a helicopter and they had definitely never ever been off the ground before. Their wide-eyed stares out the window were so funny to watch. As we approached the camp, the pilot decided to dive down at the bushes and trees near where he needed to land to scare away any rebels who might be hiding and could shoot us down easily. The Disneyland rides had nothing on these dives in and out. Grace and Stephen loved every second of it and were scared at the same time.

We finally landed, and as we got off, the refugees were all gathered together, staring at us. When you line up close to 18,000 people in front of you from horizon to horizon, you have an instant feeling of, *How in the world am I ever going to get these people the help they so desperately need?*

We walked through the camp and saw the dead, wounded, sick, and starving people. This included the babies, the old, and everyone in between. The water supply consisted of two shallow water holes with dark gray, filthy water in them. There was no firewood and only a small amount of medicine. The first thing I saw that we needed to do was to get some sort of food supply within a few days. The second thing was to get medicine and medical service by building and supplying a field hospital. The third thing was to get two bore holes drilled, one at each end of the camp. I knew that the bore holes would be the hardest to get done very quickly.

The whole time we were on the ground walking around, it was pouring rain, but just as we were about to fly out, it quit. I asked the pilot if he could fly over our little clinic and see how much damage the rebels had done to it when they attacked and took it over. They had now left, so it was safe to fly over it. The pilot said he would try, but if it started getting too dark, he would have to head straight back for his base. I agreed and we took off. The darkness came on us quickly, and just as we were turning away, we flew over a family compound where I knew all the inhabitants. I realized the rebels had attacked that compound and killed my friends. It hurt me so much that I cried hard all the rest of the way back.

We landed back in Soroti where we started our flight, and Stephen stayed and ministered to the village refugees he had there in town. Grace and I headed back to Jinja to get things rolling on meeting these needs. When I got back and shared what the camp was like, how hurting the people really were, and what had happened to the people we knew very well, everyone stopped and cried and prayed.

Sunny had good news for me from our home church—there were some funds for the refugee camp, with more to come. The next day, Samaritan's Purse called and told me that they had ten thousand dollars for me, plus thirty 20'x100' heavy blue plastic tarps with which to cover the field hospital. I took some of the money and began purchasing medicine. We also started making metal beds, IV stands, desks, chairs, cabinets, bedding, lanterns, poll timber, and anything else we could think of that we might need. Soon more money came from home. We received the funds just in time to pay for the drug order we had ordered on faith, hoping the funds would be there when it was due.

When we got everything together, we notified the general and told him that we now needed a heavily-armored escort for our truck into the camp on the road through rebel-held territory. He said they were short on personnel but would work something out to get us there safely. We loaded the rest of the supplies on our rented truck and headed out for Soroti, where we would be picking up our military escort.

The military in a third world country is quite different from what it is in America. You never know where you might find them once they have gone outside the major cities as they have very few bases. We ended up finding them in a big old two-story house they were using temporarily for the general's headquarters.

We waited hours before we got to see the general, but it was well worth it because he gave us two armored tanks for our escort. He could only spare a few men, or else his headquarters would become vulnerable to attack. He warned us that the rebels would definitely want to attack to get the medical supplies if he only sent soldiers, but he did not want us to be so vulnerable. That is why he gave us two tanks.

Wow! Two tanks sounded awesome to me, so I said, "Thank you, sir, and we do really appreciate your concern in providing us with tank escort."

Two hours later, the first tank showed up and the other an hour later. They briefed us on how they wanted us to position our truck and at what distance to follow them. After all was set, we headed out down a very dusty, pot-holed, old village road.

Some fear came over us once we got deeper into rebel territory and began seeing burned-out cars, trucks, and buses alongside the road. We knew we really were in it up to our ears when we came upon a vehicle still smoldering from a recent attack. We almost got whiplash trying to look everywhere at the same time, hoping we did not see a rebel, and if we did, that we could get away fast enough. We were covered with the dirt from the tank in front of us because its tracks threw clouds of dust into the air and we seemed to be their target.

All we could say was, "Tanks for the dust, thanks." About halfway to the camp, the tank in front stopped, turned around, came back, and stopped by us. The driver told me that the second tank that was riding behind us had broken down about five miles back and they must go back and protect them. We thought, *Protect them! What about us?* We did not have any weapons to defend ourselves with, that was for sure. Off down the road went our protection, and there we sat deep in the middle of rebel territory, looking at each other and wondering what might happen if they did not come back soon.

The Bible clearly tells us in 1 Thessalonians 5:17 to be continually in prayer. We made that verse become literally alive and true. The very fervent prayer going up made the dust feel like fresh air. We sat there for about an hour, hoping and praying that someone or something would come by with some help for us.

Finally, looking down the road ahead of us, we saw a man come out of the bush about a block ahead and start walking in our direction. Rebels sometimes wear a uniform, but at other times they are in plain old clothes. Therefore, we were very concerned that this guy might be a rebel spy. Pastor Stephen recognized the man as one of his friends from near our clinic area. We all breathed a sigh of relief, and even more so when the man said there was a small detachment of soldiers camped about five miles down the road ahead of us. At that, we drove down the road very slowly to not raise any dust and become a target for the rebels, should they be nearby.

When we arrived at the small outpost, we could see that these poor soldiers had very little to protect themselves from the environment. It was monsoon season, and they were getting drenched when it rained, with no cover to get under. So I took some of the donated tarps and divided a couple of them up into 5'x5' squares so each soldier would have some protection. The head officer there was thrilled at our giving these men the tarps. He said that most of them had been too sick to go out on patrol, which had allowed the rebels to wreak havoc in the area. He gave me a big Ugandan hug and then he and some of the other soldiers lifted me up on their shoulders and danced me around for a few minutes. Everybody was happy and laughing wildly. We were celebrating, too, because this surely meant they would make sure we were safe for the night.

About ten in the evening, the two tanks showed up; one tank was towing the other. After we found everyone a place to sleep for the night, I got into the cab of our truck and tried to get some much-needed sleep. A downpour came, along with high wind to make it worse. We had tied one of the tarps over the supplies on the truck, but the wind was ripping it off. I tried to replace it, but the wind was too strong for me, so I got back into the truck and started praying. Drugs are no longer good if they get wet. These drugs were in cardboard boxes, so I thought we might lose the whole bunch.

I didn't get much sleep because I prayed most of the night. The next morning I got out of the truck a bit hesitantly, thinking the worst-case scenario was going to be awaiting me. The first look at the boxes sent my heart sinking down to my shoes—they were all wet, soggy, and limp. But as I opened and checked some of the worst-looking boxes, everything in them was completely dry. Not one ounce of medicine was lost, praise God. Prayer is so powerful because God is always listening and caring about all that goes on in everyone's lives.

About eight-thirty in the morning, with only one tank left for our escort, we headed out toward the camp. We had to pass through two small townships on the way. The first had a couple of rebels in it, but they took off running into the bushes. The second was a bit scarier, because the tank suddenly stopped and swung the turret around, pointing it to a sign down the road behind which we could see some rebels hiding. The soldiers riding on top of the tank jumped off and ran toward the rebels. Just as they jumped off, more rebels came out of hiding and took off running toward the bushes, as did the ones down the road. By this time, we were wide-eyed and praying a hundred miles an hour. Just as fast as we had stopped, we took back off, this time much faster than before, so we made sure we kept our truck's speed up with that of the tank. We finally cleared those areas and arrived at the refugee camp.

Thousands of people stood at the edge of the camp shouting and dancing when they saw the truck coming with help. It was an awesome sight to see and hear, let alone be a part of bringing it to them. We had some serious difficulties as we tried to get the truck unloaded. People tried to take stuff right off the truck and run off with it. I quickly got some soldiers to stop them. They raised their guns in the air and let off a few rounds. At that, everyone dropped what they had taken, and we quickly collected it and regained control. We had also brought some medical staff, plus workers to help build the field hospital, distribute the medicines, and distribute the tarps after they were cut to the right size. There were so many people waiting to get treatment that it looked like we were giving away a new car or something.

Sadly, people brought babies who had already died and asked us to help them. The hurt was too great at seeing the pain in their hearts when we had to dash their hope. We saw people whom rebels had shot while they were out looking for water or food. Some of these were very small children, five to nine years old, and the rebels had still shot them. There is no reason for this type of atrocity anywhere.

Knowing about these terrible things is difficult enough, but there are even worse things that these rebels did to their captives. When you see these things, you are left with nightmares for a long time. The sickening thing they did most often was to mutilate the body while the victim stayed alive. They cut off the ears, lips, eyebrows, eyelids, and nose. They also cut off the women's breasts and the men's privates and turned the victims loose, calling it intimidation tactics. This was supposed to keep people from supporting the government or from telling where the rebels were. How stupid can they be? When you see one of these people so tortured, you surely would know that the rebels were in that area. They also abducted small children and took them to an airfield in Sudan where they traded them for weapons provided by a well-known Arab country. This country then sold them as house-slaves, never to be heard of again.

We live in such a "I don't care about your problems" society in America. We have no desire to hear or know what is going on in other, less fortunate peoples' lives—especially in third world countries like India or Uganda. We might say, "Poor, poor people; someone ought to do something about it." Hey, maybe you should be the one to help make the difference by simply going and teaching righteousness or by supporting those whom God has already placed in the middle of these peoples' great pain. When you simply do nothing, you are really not listening to God and His Word. Please go to the Word and investigate what God says about your needing to get involved in other peoples' sufferings.

When nightfall came, the captain came to me and said we needed to leave because the rebels had moved closer to the camp and had shut off our normal return road. He also stated that they must have found out that an American was there and they would want to capture me to embarrass the government. The captain wanted us to get out of there as fast as we could, so we jumped into the truck, got in line with some of the other relief trucks that had been waiting a few days for an armed escort, and left. We headed back a different way from the way we'd come in, and it was a very long way back. I found out later that just before we left the camp, the captain had been notified that the rebels had cut off the road we'd come in on. The back way took almost all night to travel from one

N. Uganda refugee camp, Jo on left, and Sunny on the right playing with all the orphans

refugee camp to another. The military also needed to drop off supplies and ammo to their troops along the way.

Sunny and a visiting lady named Jo had kept us busy playing with the kids from camp to camp. They screamed, laughed, and ran everywhere we went. Luckily, we had topped off our gas before we left Soroti on the way to the camp, and we made it back with the gas gauge dead on empty. The next day, after some very much-needed sleep and a hot bath, we headed back to Jinja to find some peace and rest.

Chapter 15

Golf, Snakes, Demons, and Monitor Lizards

I HAVE HEARD MANY a fishing story in my lifetime, and almost as many golf stories. But these stories are here to tickle you just a little, and they are true.

I had never played golf before in my life, but the doctor who was working on my neck pain wanted me to take up golf. He said the rotation therapy was just what my neck needed to help it straighten up and possibly stop paining me. So I began calling the other missionaries around our area to see if any of them had a left-handed set of clubs they might sell me. The missionary community tried to get together at least once a month for a pot luck supper, some devotional time, and singing. It was at one of these meetings that I asked again, and this time a Baptist missionary said he had some left-handed clubs in his container that I could check out. I made a sweet deal on them—he just gave them to me. The clubs were old, but who cares when you do not know how to play anyway?

With clubs in hand, I jumped into my van and headed for the golf course. Third world golf courses can give a golfer many excuses for shooting badly. An example would be the signs that read, "You get a free drop when you land in a hippo track." I have yet to find a hippo track on the course. The grass in the roughs is nearly knee high; in the fairways it's just below the ankle during dry season, and over the ankle in the rainy season. The greens are seldom watered, so if it doesn't rain, you play on a mostly dry surface. When it's rainy, you putt through a deep pile rug, with bumps everywhere. It was golf at its best. Right.

These were the conditions under which I had to learn to play golf. Another problem was finding time to play. I got time off when I just walked away to grab some sanity. I guess golf could be a sanity-grabber for me.

Learning to play golf by yourself is not something I would highly recommend. I lost more balls than I found. Even when I got wise enough to hire a caddy to watch the ball for me, I still lost a bunch of balls. Eventually, I got to where I could hit the ball more than a hundred yards. Some drives even went almost two hundred yards, but finding those suckers was the fun part.

One day, my caddy and I were looking for a ball in deep grass up to our knees when he jumped about five feet into the air yelling, "Cobra, cobra!" and landing about eight feet from where he was originally standing. I said, "Let's just forget that ball and let this cobra have it as his trophy for the day." I never went into deep rough looking for a ball again.

One time, when I was on a very long par five hole, my drive was a big one and landed about halfway down the fairway in a sand trap. When the caddy got to the sand trap, he started jumping up and down yelling, "Demon, demon, demon!" and came running back and hid behind me. I could not help but laugh; it was such a funny sight.

When I approached the sand trap, some dirt came flying out of a big hole in it, so I moved in a little more carefully now. As I looked into the hole, I could see that it was just a big female monitor lizard which had dug back into the sand to lay her eggs. These monitor lizards are between six and ten feet long, vicious, and can cover ground pretty fast. I sneaked back up behind my caddy, and being the jokester that I can be at times, grabbed him from behind and pretended I was going to throw him to his demon. He almost killed me trying to get away, and he was so scared that he wet himself. Then I really felt bad for doing it, and I gave him a big tip to try to offset my horseplay at his expense. Shame on me, but it was funny.

Playing golf in Uganda is also an experience of beauty. The Nile River runs right next to the course. Palm trees are everywhere and many other flowering trees grow abundantly. Marabou storks are on every green. You should not look up under a palm tree, though, as the giant fruit bats nesting there dropped waste on you by the tons. These bats had wingspans of eighteen inches or more. Some Ugandans ate them, while others think they are demons.

I met some very nice people while playing golf and did a lot of witnessing to them. This was especially true with the young caddies who were not attending school as they should. I explained their great need for a good education and for Christ in their lives. Some of them came to our church and eventually gave their lives to the Lord.

Chapter 16

The Handicapped and "Teka-Tekas"

MISSIONARIES ARE ASKED to serve in a wide variety of ministries. Granted, you cannot fulfill everybody's desires for help, but you should at least evaluate and carefully consider each request in prayer.

A group of handicapped people came to our house to see if we would come and start a church near where most of them lived. We prayed and felt led to at least test it out. They also asked me to come see some of the projects they were making to earn income for the group. I set up a time to meet with them and let them go on their way.

The Lord began working on my heart from the very beginning to help them, and He showed me what was needed. They welcomed me with a large crowd. This is not uncommon since they want you to feel special and consider supporting them in some way. They brought me a Coca-Cola and the items they were making, like handwoven hats made from banana leaf fibers, chair seats from the same kind of fibers, and straw mats. None of these items were making them very much money, and they needed to find a project that could generate enough income to offset their deep financial needs. We talked for two hours about all their problems, about where they actually lived, how many kids and wives they had, and on and on.

The reason I asked how many wives they had was to find out if they are born again Christians or not. Christians in Uganda can only have one wife, but traditional villagers could have as many as they could support and Muslims could have up to four. This is not really adhered to, however, as they just keep adding them on. After that meeting, I felt I had enough information to go and pray about things. We would then try to see if we could find some way not just to help them, but to do it in such a way that they would be able to help themselves. This way, they would gain some pride and self-sufficiency.

I had never worked around or with the handicapped before and was at a loss at first. But God never fails in giving you a word of wisdom, especially when it is going to be helping someone who is less fortunate. Being from New Mexico, and with the Mexican culture on display daily in my life, I remembered some of their crafts that were for sale in stores. The one that came to mind as a project to consider and that they all could be involved in making was the Mexican yo-yo. The Mexican yo-yo is made from wood and has a bigger round top with a peg sticking up and with a longer handle. One end of a string is attached to the round top and the other end to a piece of wood that looks like a small cup with a hole in it the size of the peg. You swing it up, trying to get the small cup to land on top of the wooden peg sticking up on top. These toys are fun and very colorful. Most importantly, people would buy them, and they could be made cheaply.

The big hump to get over was how to make it in such a way that they could each have a part in its construction. These people did not have the ability or money to afford a wood lathe. Therefore, another medium would have to be used to make the yo-yos. I remembered that the African cows had big horns, and they were plentiful at the stockyards.

I went and got a couple of horns, came home, and began trying to make a few types of yo-yo's from them. To my surprise, it was not at all that hard once I started cutting off the tip of the horn. I cut it about ten inches down from the tip; then, two inches up from the smallest end, I cut to make the smaller part that would be swung up and into the larger opening of the remaining horn.

We filed them smooth and then attached one end of a two-foot string to the smallest piece and the other end to the big open end of the horn. Grabbing hold of the big part with the opening upright, I began swinging the small part to make it swing up and over the top—just hard enough to make it drop into the opening. It took some practice before I got the hang of it, but after that I had a blast trying to do better than the time before.

I then went as far as finding a way to make the toys colorful. This took some doing since the people cannot afford thinners, paint, or paintbrushes.

The Handicapped and "Teka-Tekas"

We came up with a dipping method. First, the two pieces needed to be dipped into varnish and then hung up to dry. Second, the small end of the biggest piece was dipped down two inches into yellow paint and hung on a drip tray to dry. Thirdly, it was then dipped in some red paint about an inch and a half, and hung up to dry. On the last step, it was dipped only one inch into black paint, and then hung up to dry. Uganda's flag is red, black, and yellow. That is why we chose these three colors.

When I took it to them, they went wild with excitement. They also spent more time having fun with them than listening about how to make them. So I let them enjoy themselves for a while and had a few laughs to go along with their fun.

We spent many hours evaluating each person's handicap, and then I developed methods and tools for them to be a part of making the Teka-Tekas, which is Ugandan for "Put in-put in." That is as close a term as I could find in their language for this type of yo-yo. When I brought all the equipment to them and unloaded it, people came from all around to see what was going on. By the time we got it all set up, we had quite a crowd gathered around us. Some real joy came rushing upon us as we watched each person start working with the equipment we had designed for them. They were smiling at just being able to be a part of something like everyone else. They began singing, laughing, and some even cried over their new project. They did not waste any time getting the system down pat and began producing some Teka-Tekas to sell.

Within a week, they had about eighty ready, and they looked great. Needless to say, I bought the first ten for myself and still have some today. Since none of them had ever sold to outside outlets before, I needed to go with them to get things started. We ended up with fifty or so outlets, and orders for two hundred of our Teka-Tekas. I went with them on their first delivery run and watched as they had fun showing people how to work them.

Things went on well for a while, but then it became obvious they were using me to do most of the legwork. It was beginning to interfere with many of my other ministries, so I called another meeting and set things straight about my role in their new making, selling, and distributing. They looked a bit puzzled at my new stance but soon got the message that it was now up to them to succeed. I guess you could say it was time to sink or swim. The whole project lasted about a year, and they grew lazy making them on time and failed to get product to their customers. They mainly did not want to spend their money on the travel it took to sell them and ate it up in other ways.

The church, on the other hand, was doing very well and showing steady growth. We found a man in the group who was taking his walk with the Lord very seriously, so we allowed him to enter our school of ministry. He did very well and was later ordained as a pastor. He now pastors Calvary Chapel for the handicapped, and it is still growing.

We also helped the handicapped with their polio deformities. When the medical people went around to villages to inoculate people against polio, they all thought it was going to be with needles. They were afraid of needles, due to AIDS being transferred that way in their country. Doctors and nurses in third world countries are more interested in making money any way they can than in sanitation, so they reuse the needles many times over.

Because of this, many people got polio and have suffered greatly from all the resulting deformities. We were told about a doctor in Kampala, the capital, who specialized in helping these polio victims. We loaded up three of the worst cases we had and went to see him. He checked them over and reported to me that two of them could be helped with only two or three operations, but the third one would need up to ten operations and would take a couple of years.

We scheduled them on his list and prayed for him and his wonderful gift and work. He worked wonders on each person we brought to him and was always excited to see our patients and us. This same doctor was killed by a car thief one day just as he arrived to work. The thug walked up and shot him dead, threw his body out on the ground, and drove off. Like I said earlier, the thug problem is a really serious one and not to be taken lightly.

When confronted with a decision as to whether to do a ministry or not, you should always take the time to pray first. God is longsuffering and is in no hurry. Since this is true, you should not be afraid to get involved. You should then let some time pass in testing the ministry to see whether you should continue it. Sometimes it is meant for someone else to do and not you.

I got the prison ministry from a Baptist missionary. I went for a visit to prisons with him, and when he saw that God was using me in a powerful way and men were coming to Christ, he turned and said, "You should be doing this and not me." He explained that he had not been able to get the men interested before, and it was obvious to him why God had him invite me that Sunday.

Remember what I told you about Jesse and Beverly when they came out to prisons with us on their first visit. Even then, it was obvious that they should be the ones running the prison program from then on and not Sunny and me. Believe me, it is not so hard to step down when you remember that all ministries belong to God and not to you. When people place their own names on the ministry they are called to do, it makes me worry whom are they giving the glory to. Would they release it to others if God needed that to be done? All glory belongs to God, forever and ever.

Chapter 17

Some Game Park Experiences

NAKURU GAME PARK in Kenya is by far our favorite place to go and see wildlife. The park has a wide variety of landscapes that the game tends to hide in or feed nearby. The only animal that is not there is the elephant. Other than that, most of the other types of African wildlife are abundant and you do not go very far without seeing something exciting.

One time, we saw a female rhinoceros and her small baby. They were about a half mile away but came our way while grazing. We sat there for over an hour, hoping for an up-close encounter to photograph. The rhino finally walked within thirty feet of the front of our van, and the baby turned to face us. He lowered his head, plowed his front feet into the ground, and made movements with his head that looked like he was going to charge us and try to do some terrible damage. It was a wonderfully hilarious sight to watch—such a little guy making as if he were a giant we should fear. The mama kept a steady eye on us the whole time. Needless to say, she was not little at all; in fact, she was about as big as our van.

Another time, we came upon some lions very early in the morning, just before the sun was fully out. The first one we saw was about fifty feet ahead of us, lying in the road. The sunlight was barely breaking through the trees, and a heavy mist was hanging over the whole area. As we watched, the lion got up and slowly strolled our way. The sunlight and mist were perfect for an awesome photo, so I grabbed the opportunity and snapped some good shots.

Soon four more lions showed up and began hanging out very close to our van. They were so close that you did not make the mistake of leaning out the window too far and becoming their breakfast. Another beautiful lion came and laid in the grass just a few feet away from me. He tilted his head up toward heaven with such a reverent look on his face, as if he were saying, "Yes, Lord, You are the only true King," or maybe, "Thank you, Lord, for the missionary breakfast."

This picture and many others are framed and hanging in our living room. Another lion lay down near Sunny, and she talked to him through the window. Without my noticing her, she leaned way outside the window and snapped some pictures of him. He did not like it at all and turned and growled at her. This made her quickly recoil back into the van.

She scared me so badly when I saw how far out the window she had been leaning that I began yelling at her for putting herself in danger. She means so much to me, and the lion could have leaped that far before she could have even responded. He would have had her for breakfast, while I would have had to sit there helplessly watching. She knew she scared me, that's for sure.

The male lions kept marking out the territory all around our van, as if to say, "These are our meal tickets, everyone else stand back." Believe me, I would never want to meet any size lion in the wild. They all look like they are hungry, mean, short-tempered, and unafraid of anything or anyone. Call me a coward, but a Daniel I am not.

We also saw leopards and panthers. Some lay in trees, while others ran in the bushy areas. These cats are not as plentiful as the other cat families, yet they are every bit as beautiful, tough-looking, and dangerous.

Queen Elizabeth Park always has excitement in store for you, as I have shared in other chapters. But I have a snake story in which Sunny got a chance to yell back at me. We had been looking for game for about an hour without seeing anything but warthogs after warthogs. As we came around a bend in the road, lo and behold, coming out of the bush was a python. When we first saw it, only the head and about a foot of the body showed. The road was a good twelve feet across, and it just kept coming out. Even when its head entered into the bush on the other side of the road, there was still more snake in the bush on the other side. This snake had to be at least eighteen feet long. My adrenaline was pumping wildly as I jumped out and ran up near it and began taking pictures. Sunny was

Giraffe in Nukuru, Kenya game park

screaming at me to get back in the van. The snake then turned and looked straight at me. I got the message and booked it back to the van. It was a very exciting moment for me to remember, though it was dumb of me to get out of the van.

Monkeys are not at all as you see them on TV or in the movies. They can be extremely mean and can slip up and bite you, jump up on you, or grab whatever you are carrying. You definitely should not turn your back on them. Baboons are scarier, larger, and more dangerous than any monkey. Here is a funny little story about a nurse named Eve, who was a bit on the heavy side. Eve was with us on a trip, and we pulled into a gas station near the game park. I had walked away to look at some carvings in a grass hut nearby. The man there jumped up suddenly and yelled, "Look out!" and indicated our vehicle. When I looked, a big colorful male baboon was sneaking up behind Eve, who was busy bending over looking into her purse on the front seat.

I started yelling as I ran toward her, finally managing to get her to stand up. She quickly turned around and faced the baboon. What happened next is the funny part. She did not show one ounce of fear and went on the offensive. She started for the baboon, kicking at him like a place kicker in a football game—kick, step, kick, step—as the baboon jumped up backward, trying to keep her from making contact. Eve did this for about fifteen feet until the station attendant ran up as if he had a stone in his hand and drew back. The baboon, seeing him draw back, took off running full speed in the other direction. I guess he had nailed the baboons a few times before. This was frightening on one hand but absolutely hilarious on the other. We all had a good time laughing about it when it was over.

Another memorable incident was when Sunny and I got close to a big bull elephant. He was about forty feet away from where we had stopped to look at him. I was sitting outside the back window on top of the spare tire leaning onto the roof of our little Suzuki Jeep with my feet inside. My elbows rested on top of the roof as I held the camera in my hands. I wanted to get the elephant to turn and face me with his ears fully extended and trunk raised.

Mister smart guy Jay decided to clap his hands very loudly and then grab the camera and start shooting pictures. The clapping part worked very well. The elephant turned and snorted, threw his ears out, and moved in our direction. Sunny, seeing him start our way, took off down the road, thus throwing me backwards as I was sitting partially out the back window. My toes were caught up in the roof, but the rest of my body was dangling out the back just inches off the ground. I was yelling, but Sunny thought I was yelling that he was getting closer, so she drove even faster. Finally, I got wise enough to only yell, "Stop, stop, please just stop!" She finally stopped and came running back to help me get out of my predicament. When we both had calmed down a little, we began laughing. It was actually very funny in the end but not while I was dangling out the back.

The last game story I would like to share with you is about some rats. We were still living on Lubogo Road in Jinja, and we were enjoying our evening devotion times. We kept hearing a noise coming from our garage, as if someone were rattling around in there. I got up and went over to the door, grasped the handle, and prepared to jump into the garage to catch myself a thief.

But when I opened the door and jumped in, it only took one look and I jumped back out the door as fast as I could. What I saw was about sixty rats climbing all over the things stored in there. When they saw me, they scattered up the walls into our roof. Just the thought of sixty or so rats running around in our roof was spine-chilling. Alfred Hitchcock did not have anything on this scene. We did not waste any time the next day getting rat poison. Hearing the rats fighting over the poison blocks kept us awake at night. The rats rolled them around in the ceiling for days on end, like a soccer match. Eventually, they died out, and we got our peace back, plus some much-needed sleep.

Mission work can drain you because of what you deal with each day. Taking a break from it once in a while is good medicine. Not taking breaks can cause you to be short with people and fail to handle things as God would have you. Remember that you are the steward of all He gives you to do, so make sure you do it properly. The people you are serving are always watching what you do and will quickly tell others when you blow it. So plan well, take some time away, and you will see more abundant fruit in the process.

Chapter 18

The Blessings of Repentance

WHEN THINGS SEEM too hard to go through or you feel like running away or hiding in some corner, God brings a special blessing to cheer you up.

Maybe you remember the story from an earlier chapter about my being arrested three times because of false reports that came from someone we would have least suspected. The accusers were the co-workers who had been a part of our mission work through the first two callings, even up through the first four years of our last calling in Jinja. We had been working hard trying to get the clinic in the north built near a small village called Ogongora.

The burden on our hearts for all the suffering these poor people were going through was too much to bear. I could not find everything I needed fast enough. I wanted to get back up there to get things moving faster, but I was not gaining the headway I had expected and desired. I was in my office praying over all the issues involved and feeling somewhat helpless. I know that God can handle everything just fine, but our human nature wants to worry about things we cannot control.

A knock on my study door accompanied a voice saying, "Papa Jay, you have some visitors." I got up and went to see who it was. Surprise is what I got, and being surprised is an understatement at who was there wanting to see me. It was Rose and Robert, the couple we had to have the police remove from our home because of the danger they had become to us. They had leveled false charges to the police, causing me to be arrested three different times.

Robert and Rose were crying as they approached me, saying, "Maze, Maze, we have come to ask for yours and mommy's forgiveness. Please forgive us." This was quite a shock to us both, not just seeing them but hearing what they were saying. We gave both of them a big hug and told them that we had forgiven them years earlier, like God had required us to do. It sounds like we're trying to be very spiritual. We can say these things to people so easily, but what we are feeling deep down inside is a totally different thing. One second I was wondering what they were up to, and the next moment I wanted to cry and make them feel welcome on their visit with us.

God always wins, especially when He has a plan that is too hard for us to figure out, and this was one of those times. Robert quickly went on to tell us that they were not there to ask for their jobs back, but to ask for forgiveness and thank us for how well we had trained them in the work of ministry. They continued by telling us that they now were working with an international relief agency and were helping to bring relief to many thousands of refugees in southern Sudan. The Muslim government had chased the refugees into the barren desert to try to starve them to death.

We felt very proud of them and rejoiced at the change God had wrought in them. We had spent numerous hours training them over the years, and it was wonderful to see it all going to good use for God's glory. Sunny had taught Robert how to drive, and it was this ability that helped him get this new job. His ability to manage details and people were skills I had taught him. His employers have now made him a field manager for the district he is serving in.

We spent many more hours talking over old things, yet leaving out the negative issues to keep things on the positive side. They came back often on their breaks from Sudan, trying to get some much-needed rest from their heavy workload. Their children were mostly now in their teens and were polite and well-behaved. This surely made us feel a whole lot older. These visits were a blessing after that wonderful day.

It's wonderful how God can bring things full circle to accomplish His goals in all our lives. But the old things that happened between us years earlier did not go away easily. I found that it would take some time for more healing for that to happen.

Let me try and clarify this better for you. God is the only one Who can choose to remember no more because He is God. We as humans remember all that has hurt us in our lives, each and every detail. God tells us in Galatians 6:7 that a man reaps what he sows. This also means what has been sown that was sinful hurts us in our lives, hindering our spiritual growth. God also tells us in Ephesians 4:26, "In your anger do not sin" or "Be angry but do not sin."

We rejoiced on the one hand and were still a bit angry on the other over the terribleness of things done in the past. Forgiving someone is one thing, but forgetting it is another one altogether. God remembered the past sins of the Jewish fathers and used them to get their attention, often leading to repentance and them returning to Him. It worked for God, and it will work for us today as long as we don't beat the person who has wronged us over the head with the fact that we've forgiven him or her.

Chapter 19

The Painful Departure from Mission Service

D EPARTURE CAN BE a terrible word since it is often related to someone who has died departing this dwelling place. This is how you feel when you are leaving mission work—like a death just took place. Nothing in the world can prepare you for leaving the work that has been your life for so many years. Leaving actually feels like the death of a close family member has just taken place. The sorrow is so real and so devastating that you can hardly deal with it. The list of people you have ministered to is long. The memories are deeply cherished, never to be forgotten. The look on people's faces as you are disappearing out of their sight leaves you in tears for days on end. The tears, hugs, and stories of how much they love you and will miss you ring loudly in your ears.

When you look back at what God has accomplished through you, it blocks any attempt of the enemy to make you feel shame for any failure that occurred along the way. When we look at all the fruit that grew from hours of devoted effort standing bountifully before God's throne, we can smile and say, "Thank You, Lord, for allowing us to be a small part of it all."

The Lord asks us all to give, and He means just that—give of yourself. Listen to Luke 6:38 NIV: "Give, and it will be given to you. A good measure, pressed down, shaken together and running over, will be poured into your lap. For with the measure you use, it will be measured to you," blessing you and the ministry. Sure, God wants us to give of our finances in support of the church and missions. But that giving is meaningless unless you are letting Him use you in meeting other people's needs. Meeting other people's needs does not always mean giving money, but also giving service to them in whatever way is needed. We have never, ever been able to out-give God, not ever. When you live according to His will for you, He will provide abundantly for all your personal needs. This will be in addition to all the work He may call you to accomplish for Him.

When we were asked to take care of a refugee camp of 18,000 plus people, God provided for each and every one of those needs. He provided what was necessary to offset their hunger, what was necessary to meet their medical needs, and a good water supply to help keep them healthy. In addition, He kept us safe from the rebels while we traveled back and forth to the camp to see the work through until we were finished.

Let me share this with you to think about: no matter what work God called us to do, the enemy tried to hinder or destroy that work. This usually came from a blind side where we least expected it, and if our eyes and hearts were not set on God from start to finish, the enemy might just have won. God gave us victory, even when others thought we had failed. He continued working powerfully through us and with us to bring Him His due glory.

Praise God, we had well-trained people to take our places when we did leave—Jesse and Beverly, Ryan, and a wonderful lady named Jo, plus all our Ugandan staff. Knowing they had hearts for Uganda and the people made leaving much easier. We do, however, envy their still being there working at what we loved so much while we are not there to grasp a part of their joy.

One thing that has helped me more than I ever thought it would is all the photos and video footage taken over the years. Most of them we had not looked at since the day they were taken. When we look at them now, we get to relive the event and some of the excitement we enjoyed at that time. We get tears and feel a great loss of that daily connection to such a loving people and their needs.

Returning to America may sound like an easy thing to do, but nothing could be further from the truth. America is well known as the land of plenty, and that is an understatement. If you have never been in a place where finding what you need becomes a daily hunt, you may not grasp our frustration. You would think that when you come back and go shopping and can find what you need in just one store, you would rejoice. Believe me, we did rejoice, but not without mind-boggling frustration. Here in America, there are just too many choices to make on each purchase. There are twenty to thirty different milks, breads, canned goods, fruits, cheeses, meats, chips, cookies, soaps, medicines, toothpaste, shampoo, and even dog food. When you walk into an aisle with hundreds of items stacked high and wide, you are quickly overwhelmed in trying to make one simple choice. We finally adjusted after a few months and became just like everybody else.

Another thing to consider upon your return is the need to find a job or else starve to death. If you are with a denominational church group, you might not have to face this difficulty because you have a retirement budget waiting for you. We, however, were with a nondenominational church group with little to no planning for retirement from mission work available.

This means that everybody stops supporting you shortly after you are back in the states. As a result, you are left wondering which way to turn to survive. Add the fact that I was sixty-five years old when we returned and people are not anxious to hire you at that age for a decent wage. We had a little savings to help us get started, but when you have nothing at all to start with materially, that money does not last long. You have to buy clothes, furniture, bedding, dishes, pots and pans, silverware, and, of course, transportation, in addition to finding a place to live. Thank God we had some dear friends who jumped in and helped offset a lot of those needs. As I have said repeatedly, God always out-gives our efforts for Him.

Our support stopped within just a few months, and we became desperate to find jobs. I got a job as a security guard, and Sunny went to work for a home care firm at just a little over minimum wage. Still, God made sure our needs were met at the end of the month.

After about a year, God placed it on our hearts to move to Corpus Christi, Texas. After much prayer, we stepped out in faith and moved to south Texas. I had a serious medical problem arise on the way—an infection in my prostate that sent me to an emergency room in the middle of the night. With much work, we convinced the medical team to let us pay them from Corpus Christi later. The move was a big step for us since we had no jobs waiting for us and had made a down payment on a home on Oso bay in Corpus Christi with the remainder of our little savings. Here we were again with little money in our pockets but trusting that God would guide us to jobs to meet our needs and to a good church to attend.

When we arrived at our new home, it was a mess. The previous owners had done little to no cleaning when they moved out. They had had live-in cats, and the urine smell filled the entry. The first few days were spent cleaning and making it livable. After that, the furniture arrived in a drop-off trailer we had to unload.

I just sat on the trailer ramp and prayed for God to send me some help. Within a few minutes, a young man rode up on a bicycle and asked if I needed help unloading the truck. "Yes, sir, I sure do, my friend," I replied. With that, he went and got another young friend, and they came and did most of the work. Turns out both had been out of work for a while and really needed money for food and rent. I hired them to put up a fence and do some other yard work, and their need was met, as was ours. God does answer our prayers.

Sunny did not take long to make our new home a cozy place to come home to. She has such a wonderful touch in making a home a real home, no matter where we have lived.

The job searching turned into months before I finally found a job that paid enough to help pay our bills. Sunny got the same job she had in Albuquerque—taking care of the elderly. I began working at a substance abuse treatment facility, taking care of drug- and alcohol-dependent people sent from the court.

This is not what I was expecting to find for work. But when you ask God to place you where you can be used to the maximum of your abilities in helping others, He will place you in one that will test you to the max. God has allowed me to lead many of these hurting people to Christ and I could not have asked Him to use me any better.

We still struggle with our finances, although we are beginning to see the light at the end of the tunnel of our debts. God has supplied what we have needed, as He always does. He means what He says when He tells us not to put our trust in man, but in every word that proceeds from the mouth of God. We have continued in our deep devotion to Him without fail. He has never left us nor forsaken us, and He has been our comfort when others have failed or abandoned us. He has always been our Comforter when no one was in sight to help wipe away our tears. He is the faithful One in whom we trust, as He truly is our Lord and our God.

We suggest that you plan ahead for retirement better than we did. God gives funding for the whole need, not just for handing out for the needs of others. Therefore, it is not wrong to set aside funding for yourself for retirement down the line. Even if it is not for retirement, you still should set funding aside for returning back to the States and helping you get back on your feet and back to work.

I believe what you need to do now is go to your church leaders and humbly ask for a place to start serving the needs of others. Then set aside more personal time to study God's Word daily. The same goes for having an unhindered prayer time filled with lifting other people's needs up more than your own. Give more of yourself to Him, and He will give you more of what your heart has really been searching for, which is a closer relationship with Him and His Son Jesus Christ.

We can only hope you have enjoyed part one of this book and that it is a real help to you in finding your place in mission service, wherever it may be. Please continue to read on and enjoy the knowledge and wisdom you will find in part two.

It was our pleasure to share this with you. May it enhance your abilities in service for His glory. Now may God bless you, as you bless Him, while serving the needs of others. To God be the praise and glory forever and ever, amen.

Part Two

The Making of
a Missionary

Chapter 20

What a Missionary Really Is

THE TERM *MISSIONARY* does not appear in Scripture. Yet viewed as an office or position in the church, such as the offices of evangelist, pastor, or teacher all rolled into one, as they serve in all three positions. What it has come to mean in the English language usage is anyone, be they evangelist, pastor, teacher, or co-servant, who is sent into a foreign land or culture. The biblical offices of the church are the same, regardless of their geographic location. By holding a church office, the missionary is differentiated from a Christian going out short-term to give the gospel in a foreign land. The big differences are that the missionary is holding a long-term church office, the other is just visiting.

Many churches take portions of their congregation on one- to two-week "missionary" trips. These are short-term and do not transplant a church office into a foreign land. This is not the use of the word missionary that we are discussing in this book.

Webster's dictionary defines a missionary as:

> One who is being sent out, or given a charge of specific duty or service to render. Religiously explained as a "team effort" for the spread of religion in a foreign land, or culture.

The key piece of information here is that it is a sending out into a foreign land or culture, not just a going out. There is a specific reason, or goal, to be accomplished in order to please the one (or group) who has sent you out. Therefore, we need to make sure who is the one who is sending us out—is it God or man?

Genesis 1:28 was the first missionary calling. "God blessed them, and God said to them, 'Be fruitful and multiply, and fill the Earth, and subdue it; and rule over the fish of the sea, over the birds of the sky, and every living thing that moves on the earth." We know Adam did as God asked and named all the animals, plants, and everything in his sight. Sadly, Adam did not follow all that God had told him to do in completing the calling given to him.

Remember this well—when God gives you a calling, make sure you know what He wants you to do in that calling, and then do not detour from it. Do not fail to follow His instructions.

Another calling God gave was to Noah in Genesis 6. Sin had grown out of control, and mankind was doing evil in the sight of God. Sons of God were marrying the daughters of men, and wickedness grew to an abomination to the Lord. God called righteous Noah out from amongst the people and gave him a mission to build an ark large enough to carry his family and, two by two, all the different kinds of animals, birds, and creeping things.

Noah did exactly as God commanded him. But he had to accomplish it with much opposition and ridicule from the people. Remember, not everyone is going to agree with you on what God has called you to do. Your opposition can even come from church leadership, just like Christ had against Him. You can have your friends and family stand up and say you should not go for whatever reason. Your main opposition will definitely come from the enemy of God and man—the devil. Because Noah did exactly as God asked of him, his whole household was saved through the great flood, and mankind is here today because of that obedience.

Exodus 3 shows us a missionary calling that everyone is very familiar with—the calling of Moses. Moses is a good example of God calling a missionary in a very unusual and miraculous way. Moses received his calling from God through a burning bush. He was a bit hesitant and he even argued; yet finally did what God had told him to do. Because of his obedience, the whole Jewish nation was released from captivity and led to the Promised Land, but not without many hindrances and difficulties along the way.

God may speak to you in some unusual ways, but He tells you to test the spirit to see if it is from Him. If it is not against God's Word, you can be reasonably sure you are headed in the right direction. Proverbs 11:14 gives important advice that we should not forget, "Where there is no guidance the people fall, but in an abundance of councilors there is victory."

Do not try to be a know-it-all and then get embarrassed when you have to return home a failure. Get people praying for God to clearly show you His will. Prayer is a must have safety valve, and it is your connection to His power in all that you do for Him. Remember, you are weak; He is strong, not the other way around.

David is another man whom God called as a missionary, as found in 1 Samuel 17. David is a great example that God can use anyone, at any time, to fulfill His desires for mankind.

David was only a young boy when God gave him his first calling and the power to defeat the giant Goliath. The men who were supposed to be Israel's great warriors were standing around shaking in their boots, too afraid to go out to fight the giant. David, knowing in his heart and spirit that God had sent him to destroy the giant, went out to the battlefield and, without any fear of the unknown, defeated the giant. Without God you can be badly beaten up and discouraged, and you can return home with little desire to ever return to the foreign mission field again. One way you do not want to come home is in a body bag, and that means you are dead. So increase your odds of surviving during dangerous times by being very sure it is God's calling and not your fleshly desires at work in you.

I know this firsthand as you have read in part one—God can and will have His victory in all that might come your way whether it's something simple or a life-threatening task. Miracles are far more common on the foreign mission field than they ever will be back at home. The reason they are lacking at home is that at home we do not go past our abilities or our safety zone. On the foreign mission field, you cannot always just pick up and drive safely home. You are quite often put in circumstances that you are not able to control or, in your human ability, handle on your own. The situations can be beyond man's abilities and land in the hands of Almighty God for Him. I found that this happens quite often to all foreign missionaries. Some of God's miracles are so small you might miss them if you are not watching very closely. Others can be so mind blowing that you sit for days in awe at what God did for you to experience and see His greatness in. I still find myself weak when I think of some of the miracles God has brought us through. I know we will experience even more of Him, especially when we trust Him strongly enough to go do whatever He places in our paths, no matter what it might be.

Then we have the apostles in the New Testament, who all had a God-given calling to complete. They came from a wide range of backgrounds and abilities. They all served Him willingly, most even died while accomplishing their callings. Did they worry about the money or complain about what they were called to do? No way. Except for one, Judas Iscariot, they all stepped up to the line and went for it.

Who, besides them, was blessed in the end for their dedication to their calling? You got it—you and I and the entire world. You might be used by God in such a way that will shake up a whole nation, or it might be helping an elderly couple who cannot mow their lawn. Remember, if you are not faithful in the small things, then do not expect God to call you to do anything big for Him. God watches to see how humble you are while you are serving in the body of your home church. You do things for God because He has shown you they need to be done, and you should do it humbly, without complaining, all for His glory, not yours.

The types of missionaries

From my experience as a foreign missionary and from serving in the church body while at home, I have learned that there is more than one type of missionary God calls upon. God can never be stuffed into some small box where we can know all He is going to do in our lives, the church, or any part of the world. Ministry needs and the ways to bring people into a deeper relationship with Christ are limitless. Just look in your own church—are all pastors, teachers, ushers, or worship leaders? Read Ephesians 4:11-16 and all of 1 Corinthians 12. These verses also apply to the mission field because God has set up one order for His church—regardless of its location—called servanthood.

The first missionary type is what I call a "visionary missionary, and an evangelist." This is the one God calls to start the work and to oversee it so that it continues to grow. Visionary missionaries are also the ones who begin training people in God's Word and work so they are properly trained to take their places someday. They do this because God has moved upon their hearts to go to new fields where others have not yet been or have failed to complete their ministry.

In the book of Acts, the apostle Paul was called by God to go to the Gentiles first, then on to other areas. Each time he trained leadership to take his place and then periodically checked back on them, making sure Scripture was being taught correctly and more souls were being added to the kingdom.

The second type of missionary is the "administrative missionary." Administrative missionaries come out and are trained to take over a work, fine-tune it by organizing all the details, and then stabilize it so it will run much smoother. Jesse and Beverly Rich, who took our places, were that type of missionary. Jesse took over the three men's prison ministries, organized them into a fine-tuned instrument, and they kept on growing steadily. Beverly did the same thing with the women's prison ministries. Between the two of them, they got better medicine and medical care and high yield seed to properly feed the prisoners, installed a mail-in Bible correspondence course, and ran an ambulance service when it was needed. Jesse got nervous when I went out to establish a new area of ministry because this was not what the Lord had mainly called him to do. Yet when it was set up, he took it and made it run better. We all have gifts and talents God gave each of us to be used by Him as He sees fit.

The third type of missionary is what I will call a "para missionary." Para missionaries fill most of the help's positions in missions. They are the ones who come alongside and take care of all the loose ends and other details that possibly would not get done properly without them. The one with the big mission vision is always too busy fulfilling what he or she believes God has said to do and cannot find the extra time to take care of the smaller details that would better stabilize the mission and help it grow. You have these in your local church assisting the pastor. They are seen washing children's toys, cleaning the church, ushering, making the tapes or CDs, running the bookstore or the radio station, being greeters, bookkeepers, office workers, or receptionists, and even leading the worship.

Missions have many, if not all these types of missionary callings as well. Some para missionaries will be at home taking care of your support, newsletters, bookkeeping, prayer warriors, and getting you there and back safely. The rest will come with you and do whatever needs to be done to help keep things running smoothly. They are priceless and deserve to be told so often.

Let's look at all three types of missionaries this way. We all know somewhat of what it takes to make a car run properly, right? There is the engine, steering wheel, transmission, brakes, tires, radiator, headlights, taillights, the body, window glass, radio, seats, rugs, temperature control gauge, and, of course, the good old speedometer. All are important and must function as they were designed to do. Without all coming together properly, you will break down and get nowhere.

Please, never forget that all gifts and callings are there for serving others and not ourselves. It takes a full team effort, working together to make things run smoothly, so you arrive at your God-given goal. In other words, this is a description of any functional church body anywhere on earth.

Am I actually a missionary?

This is a question no one should ask lightly. We all want to do one main thing, and that is to be in the will of the Lord at all times. This is especially true when you are serving somewhere you know little to nothing about. Being there in your flesh—for your glory and not God's—means you are there in your very limited power, not in His mighty power above all powers. I don't know about you, but I know I'm not some sort of super power, all knowing, can-do-anything type of person. I am weak, dumbfounded most of the time, and cannot even find my other sock in the morning. Knowing this is true, I am not going to pretend I am anything but in need of His great power, His awesome presence on and in my life at all times. Especially when the going gets tough, and believe me, as a missionary, that is quite often. You need to know God is actually in charge of your life at all times in every circumstance.

Sad to say, I have met missionaries who came to the field only because some church mission board had sent them, but not God. Don't get me wrong, not all missionaries sent out by a board are uncalled by God—most are called. What I am saying is just because they came out of some seminary and could not find a position they could fill in a church at home, they sometimes end up settling for anything to earn a paycheck. Some are there only in their power, not in God's. Some others come in other ways, with other reasons, but not because God sent them. You will know who they are very quickly; they are the ones who find all the petty things to complain about and are very critical of how others are doing their work. They often keep to themselves and avoid doing hard work or new outreaches. The other thing they seem to do quite often is to count the number of days they have left before they can retire and return home. Thank the Lord that this type of missionary is rare.

The most deadly thing about someone going out just because it's his or her desire to do so is that the person may not be under God's guidance and protective covering. Therefore, he will be relying on his own abilities to handle the unknown things that seem to come up almost daily. I personally have faced some extremely dangerous situations in serving the Lord, and I know the only reason I am here writing this today is that God intervened and brought me through those times of almost certain death. What I would suggest before you start telling anyone that you feel called to be a missionary, is to be realistic with yourself. Start by looking at how much you are actually serving in the body right now. Then you must also be realistic about how biblically mature you really are. Finally, you need to know for sure the actual location you are to serve in.

Many of those who have come up to me over the years, who thought they were called to be a missionary, had not even served one day in a servant's role in their home church. Yet, after talking to them for a few minutes, it would become obvious what they really wanted was a limelight position, to get patted on the back for being someone special. You know, "I am a missionary, please polish my throne" type of people. These are bad enough at home in the local church, but on the mission field they quickly get depressed when they find out how much hard work they will have to do daily—especially because they do not get glorified for doing the work expected of them. They are quick to get discouraged and return home, and they end up blaming the other missionaries there for their return. They are also the ones who seem to step out too often in their flesh and end up getting themselves into serious problems, dangerous circumstances, and sometimes even killed.

If you are not serving in the local body and enjoying it in an unselfish manner right now, I doubt seriously if God is the one telling you to go be a missionary. No real missionary is without an unselfish heart and life, expressed by how much he or she is humbly serving in each opportunity placed before him or her. If this is not what you know beyond a doubt is in your heart, please do not go out pretending to be called by God to be a missionary.

On the other hand, if you fit the servant category and reasonably meet the qualifications I have placed before you in this book, you can rest assured you can be used by God any place, anytime, and do a great job in building the kingdom for His glory.

If you do not fit them, please do us all a favor and stay home where you belong until you do fit them. Then you will be a blessing to those you would serve and serve with and not be the unwanted burden weighing everyone down.

Chapter 21

How Much Do You Really Know?

YOU MIGHT THINK I mean how smart you are in school—yes, to some extent, but you will need much more. Only a fool says to himself, "I know, I know, that I know," when he has no clue what he is talking about. I have met well-meaning people who have come out for a week or two, or maybe even a month, and then they go home and say they know all about being a missionary. You might ride a train, but you're not an engineer who really knows what it takes to make a real train run effectively or what to do if something terrible goes wrong. The same is true when you want to be a missionary.

Admit you will only know what others teach you and that you will not learn that overnight or in a few years. Every mission has a complicated set of guidelines, events, and schedules that change with each set of circumstances. Look at it like being a cook: you know there are many different types of meals, none put together the same way. Yet when done correctly, these meals will truly satisfy and bless the receiver. When you pretend to know how to make that meal and you do not know what you are doing, the end results can be disastrous. Sunny does not let me in the kitchen because of how little I know about cooking.

Having a good educational background has its benefits and should be considered very important, depending on where you are going to be serving and what will be required of you. Hardly a day goes by that you are not putting together some kind of program, message, or presentation. When it looks like a fifth grader did it, you will lose the trust and respect of those whom you are trying to reach. Being a short-term missionary is much easier for someone to get by with on little education and background abilities. Long-term missions are quite a different story. There are many different types of government documents you must fill out correctly, and when they are not done right, you will not get them accepted and will cause the mission work there to be hindered. You can get around this by asking who has the experience and skills to do them with you. But no one learns to walk by being carried all the time, and neither will you.

Solid Bible knowledge is necessary if you are going to have any real success at winning new souls for Christ. Foreign missions are not exempt from false religions, cults, and attacks from other missions. When this happens, you must be able to show the one seeking clarification solid biblical answers, verifying the truth he or she is hungry to hear. When you stumble around and look unsure of yourself or you are proven to be wrong, you will not gain the person's confidence back without a lot of difficulty.

You may be asked to teach a Bible class in one of the local schools. You will be required to build a strategy or a plan of action for the headmaster. Remember, you are God's representative in whatever you do in His name, and God will hold you accountable for every word you share with others. Read Acts 18:24-28; 2 Timothy 2:14-15; Titus 1:19; and Titus 2:7-8. All who share the Word of God will be held accountable for every word and will not be allowed any excuses.

Be honest with yourself—how much do you really know about your beliefs, other religions, cults, or witchcraft? When you know ahead of time that these exist where you are going to serve, go get books on them and start studying. Also, seek advice from those whom you are going to serve with; they know far better than anyone what lies ahead for you to deal with. You can never be prepared enough, nor will you stop needing to gain more knowledge from God's Word, their culture, the government there, the opposition, and on and on. God tells us throughout the Proverbs to seek wisdom, do all you can to get it, and then grasp for more. No truer words have been spoken for the missionary.

What other skills do I have?

You will become a jack-of-all-trades while on the mission field. One day you are repairing your transportation, building a church, a house, a clinic, teaching, talking to government offices, doing the plumbing, the electricity, gardening, or maybe doctoring somebody's wounds. The list is endless and so is your need to keep studying. There is always a need for a good computer person who can program, repair, develop newsletters, spreadsheets, monthly budgets, and organize the different outreaches the mission has to take care of.

I personally had to build most of our mission housing, clinics, and churches. I did this with little to no construction knowledge. What I did, though, was seek out others who were in the know, then ask them how to do things I was in the dark about. I got better at what I needed to accomplish as I gained from their wisdom and a lot of trial and error. We ended up with five churches, five houses, a two-story apartment building, and a small two-building clinic deep in the bush near the Sudan border. Admitting you do not know something is not a sign of weakness but a sign you are willing to learn. God says in Matthew 7:8, "He who seeks, shall find it."

Sunny taught cooking, quilting, and Bible studies to the ladies. She also helped run the orphan's program and met some of the medical needs that came up regularly. She also did all the budgeting for the food and household needs each month. Then she handled most of the computer work and e-mailing. Many of the girls she trained are now teachers themselves for the mission. Some have gone on to business schools or college and are able to make a living for themselves.

You must be honest with yourself and evaluate your abilities. Write out a resume, take a long look at what you have accomplished thus far in life, and share it with those who have a need to know. You do this mainly so they know where they can best use you until you gain enough experience to be used on much more difficult areas of ministry.

How much are you serving in the body now?

God does not need, nor will He use, self-seeking people who tend to raise themselves up. By this I mean those who only want a position of notoriety, the limelight, or center stage. A good name for them is "Me, me or I, I people." Missions cannot get very much done when everyone wants center stage, needing to get their share of the glory or have it their way. Teamwork always accomplishes more than individualism. Individualism sees things only one way, with only one pair of hands; thus the work is deeply limited and hindered. Remember our passage in Proverbs 11:14, "There is wisdom in an abundance of counselors."

And how about the cord of only one strand found in Ecclesiastes 4:12? God says it can be easily broken. But if you wrap two, three, or more around it, it may not be broken at all. Strength and wisdom become more abundant in numbers, not in individualism.

I cannot say this enough: God does not want or need people who are only going for self-gratifying reasons. God wants people who have true servant hearts, who do it for the needs of others. You will always find servants, serving wherever and whenever they can. You do not have to seek them out or ask them if they will help because they are right in front of you doing it.

Again, I will ask you to be honest with yourself. "What is your real reason for wanting to be a missionary?" You also need to be honest again about how you feel about serving freely in the body, starting at the lowest position and only moving up as those who are in leadership ask you to move up. Remember, do not go if you are not already serving in the body where you are attending. You should wait until you have served in the body for a good while and can find yourself actually enjoying it. If you have any reservations about serving and find it's not your cup of tea, you should stay at home.

After you begin to find enjoyment in serving others, ask God if He has another place He can use you and leave it up to Him to find the right place. Please make sure you are busy serving before you start to give being a missionary any serious thought. The dangers are too great for someone to be out there in their flesh because you will be relying only on your abilities to handle the tough times and not on the all-powerful God Who would have taken care of it. Do not be a fool—be wise, go out with a true servant heart, and you will be blessed, not discouraged, hurt, or ashamed.

Can you get along with different personalities?

This may not sound like it would be much of a problem, but when you are serving together day after day, you can begin to get on each others' nerves. We lived with another couple and a young single man in our mission house for five years before it began getting too uncomfortable for everyone.

How Much Do You Really Know?

The young man was in his twenties with his own youthful ways and had to put up with us old folks. We had different desires for music we liked. He talked a whole different language from the rest of us. However, we made it through the rough times just fine, give or take a few frustrations. He had a fair amount of Scriptural knowledge but could still have used a few more years under his belt. Jesse and I did most of the preaching, teaching, and speaking engagements. The young man was excellent at doing the youth ministries. He did the youth programs in the church and with the street kids, and helped with the orphan program.

If each person recognizes his abilities, it can work out fine most of the time. It does not work out fine when someone thinks higher of himself than he should, myself included. This happens far more than I would like, since it is actually our old human nature at work for self-expression. You do not strangle it but direct it on the right path to maturity. Some of those you work with may see or desire to do things differently from you. This can make for some unwanted friction, yet if both parties will flex a little, it can be made to work.

Here is a good example. I preached using a different approach from another co-worker. He was very methodical to the exact point of how he was taught and believed it was the only way to preach. Again, we cannot put God in some tiny little box and choke the life out of Him. I liked to use more analogies to explain what I was sharing from the Word without always having point one, two, three, or more. What matters is that the Word is taught truthfully and the listeners are well fed through the message. Our listeners were fed both ways, and the mission kept growing with solid stability. Try being more flexible and not quite so rigid—it makes for less friction.

Not only are there different personalities, but different cultures you have to deal with. You will face things that may disgust you, yet you must go about changing them slowly, not just jumping on them like a roaring lion, teeth and all, and losing them for the kingdom. For example, the men in Uganda are very used to the women having to bow down to them to greet them and having to sit on the opposite side of the church.

Some things I was much tougher on than others. I handled this by preaching a sermon about how we are not to bow down to any other god except our Lord God Almighty. Then I explained to them how making the women bow down to them was a form of the women bowing down as if the men were a god. The next thing we did was not allow anyone working for us to continue this degrading habit. Every Sunday for a while, I would not begin the service until all the men had gotten up and gone to sit with their wives. They did not roll over for me easily; it took weeks before it became the normal thing for them to do. The women bowing down would take much longer.

The local person's desires can be quite different from yours. The way they try to express themselves sometimes tends to get on your nerves, as well as how laid back they can be about doing things very slowly.

Stealing is a way of life for people who have to live in deep poverty most of their lives. You have to make sure you do not put temptation in their paths. Do not show strangers the inside of your house because they will go and tell everyone they know what they saw, the thugs will hear about it, and you will get an unwanted visit in the wee hours of the night. You must try hard not to let this stop you from loving and being patient with them. But limit what you share around them and what you trust to their care.

Remember to remain their servant, not their master. That role belongs only to God. Galatians 5:13-26 says that we should serve one another out of love, not out of fleshly gain or personal notoriety. We should be servants one unto the other, considering the other person higher than ourselves.

Can you be flexible and not rigid?

Being an American can be a big handicap when it comes to having any real patience with hindrances in our lives. We are so used to the fast food lines that we're only willing to wait a few minutes for anything. On the mission field though, you may wait for everything and have them change what they wanted from you many times over. If you're not flexible, you will explode and become overly demanding. Your American side will slip out and ruin everything gained. This type of action will get you nothing but a lost opportunity to show your supposed fruit as a Christian and not as the worldly person they see so often.

What is normal at home, more often than not, will not be the same where you will be serving. For example, you can ask for a cheeseburger and when it arrives it will be a hamburger bun with a piece of cheese on it. No matter how much you try to explain it, this is the way they believe it is supposed to be done. So you get flexible and ask for hamburger with meat, and would they please add a piece of cheese on it. By asking for it in a different way, you stay chilled and don't blow your witness.

Whenever I did a building project, being flexible was the only way I came through with any sanity left. They wanted to put down cement without mixing it thoroughly first with water, then place a one-inch layer of wet cement on top of the dry mix below. I asked them to at least try my way once just to see if they might like the way I did it any better. When they saw that it was much easier and stronger than their old way, they quickly adjusted to the new way.

What can we learn here? I let them make the decision to at least try it rather than demanding they do it my way. The reception was a more pleasant attitude, which they keep going in the workplace. They also felt respected for what they knew. They then were able to come to a decision on their own as to which was best for the task at hand. A greater respect for all concerned was obtained, and the work was finished without any hindrances.

Let these be an example in trusting God to handle the things you cannot see a way through. He is faithful to complete the good works He has begun and will finish them His way for the betterment of all. Remember, rubber bounces and bends, and rigid glass breaks easily. So be flexible, not hard-headed, and you won't crash land.

Chapter 22

Is it your Will or God's Will for you to Go?

THE JEWISH NATION could choose to listen and seek God before they went out to war. One way was sure victory, while the other meant a terrible defeat. When the leaders or the prophets sought out God's desire on a matter and did exactly as He told them to do, all was fine and the victory was theirs. When they decided to do it their own way, they ended up losing everything, including many lives. Defeat was their only trophy.

Ecclesiastes 3:8 tells us that there is "a time to love, and a time to hate; a time of war, and a time of peace." God is the one Who does the telling of who, when, why, where, and how to go to war, be it physical or spiritual, and doing so without Him means sure defeat.

With this in mind, you need to look at how my wife Sunny and I were called by God in part one and how we went about verifying it was from Him and not just of our own desires.

What is your real reason for going?

This was touched on earlier, but we need to go over it more here. When God is the one Who places a calling or desire on your heart, it will not have any selfish motives attached to it. You will have a drive that never ceases until you are actually doing what God called you to. God's callings are always service-centered, not self-serving for self-glory. Listen to Christ talking to the Pharisees and Sadducees, who were the Jewish religious leaders, in Matthew 23:5-8:

But they do all their deeds to be noticed by men, for they broaden their phylacteries, and lengthen the tassels of their garments. They love the place of honor at banquets and the chief seats in the Synagogues, and respectful greetings in the market places, and being called Rabbis [or, for our purpose, missionaries] by men. But do not be called Rabbi, for One is your Teacher and you are all brothers. (bold wording added)

Jesus told His disciples in Matthew 23:11-12:

But the greatest among you shall be your servant. Whoever exalts himself shall be humbled, and whoever humbles himself shall be exalted.

Nothing is sadder than to see a Christian who is self-seeking, lacking a true servant's heart. After Peter had denied Him three times, Christ told Peter in John 21:15-19 to first tend His lambs, then shepherd His sheep, and finally, "Peter, tend my sheep." An important point is hidden in this passage. Sheep cannot tend the shepherd; it is impossible for them to do. The shepherd receives his name because he is the one who must tend and herd the sheep. A shepherd feeds, doctors, leads them to greener pastures, and defends them against all dangers. Sheep need to be led; they cannot lead because they do not have that gift. Their role is to follow a leader, their servant-hearted shepherd.

Teams visited the mission in Uganda, and most of those who came were a blessing to have and to watch. Nevertheless, a few seem to slip into a team or a mission who are just not meant to be there. You have to correct them quite often and make them stop arguing over every decision being made. Most of the time, you have to stop their dominating talk in order to let others get a word in edgewise. They usually are very demanding and get highly upset when they do not get their own way. If you say something nice, or praise someone else's accomplishments, they pout or get jealous. Remember I told you that the entire group of God's gifts are for serving others not ourselves.

You also need to check what is going on around you every day. What are people talking to you about—is it about the same places and things that others are talking to you about? The shows you have been watching—are they showing you places that keep captivating your thoughts and desires? Does the news of devastation in some far-off land stay on your mind for days on end? Do your pastor's messages tend to point or talk about areas you have been praying about serving in? Please be wise and keep a diary of the different things you are hearing, seeing, or going through. Review them often, until you feel sure enough in your findings to set up a meeting with your church pastoral staff or missions pastor. Seek advice about what your heart is telling you, and then make sure you listen carefully to that advice.

Then take it all to God in prayer, waiting patiently for Him to sort it out for you. God will show you in His time what He has for you to do. Do not act upon this any further until you feel some real peace and assurance about it. Then go back to your pastoral staff and ask them to join in regular prayer for God's will to be done. When you get spiritual confirmation, you can begin telling people more convincingly that you believe God is calling you to go out to China, Egypt, Russia, India, Iraq, or maybe even Africa.

God will verify His calling for you if it is truly from Him. God will begin providing for every need that arises. He will do this all the way through the calling, because He said He would. Your part is to make sure you are properly prepared biblically, with all your needed documentation, luggage, and whatever else you might need to go. I am sure you want to do a great job for all concerned, so be better prepared and you will be blessed till your cup runs over.

Make sure God does the supplying

When someone has plenty of money or available support and wants to be a missionary, he or she can easily end up going out on his or her desires alone, not on God's desires. Why? People who have their own source of support will not feel the need to wait for God to supply for them because "they" have all their finances under "their" control, not God's control. Please make sure God is in control of all the facets of your calling by not taking control of any part of it. Sunny and I always sold everything we had before going out and set the money aside until we were out serving. We did this to keep anything from standing in the way of hearing God clearly to make sure He was the one providing for what is His, and to allow Him to hinder what was not of Him.

When you are a fireman, and you're caught without a fire hose in the midst of a blazing inferno, you'd better not be counting on your fleshly abilities to bring you through safely. You can blow and blow as hard as you can, but it will not die down without a power greater than the blaze. If God can divide the Red Sea (He did), or raise the dead (He did this also), or maybe heal the lame (He did that, too)—can He not save you and me? In fact, He can handle anything and everything that comes our way without fail.

You should know by now just how weak you really are in this wicked world we live in. Do you really think you want to go out on your own feeble abilities in a place where you cannot even trust the police, the doctors, or government officials? I am sure you would feel better if you had at your disposal all the power you could ever need, at any time, or at any place. Zap—and it's done. God's awesome power will provide for your every need, do the guiding, and give you your protective covering. What more could you ask for? Do not settle for your power alone and possibly pay with your life. And for what reason—pride?

When you do not allow God to be in charge, you might as well be rummaging in a trash can for your provisions. God owns the cattle on a thousand hillsides. Therefore, why dig in the trash can behind the supermarket when you are a son or daughter of the owner, who will freely provide for your every need? Remember, your own personal resources are very limited. God's resources are not, and you get to make the choice of who your supplier is going to be—God or you? Hmm, difficult, isn't it?

Is your church leadership in agreement about your calling?

This is very important to any calling, but it is not a set rule. As I shared before, God can use anyone, at any level of his or her growth, anywhere, anytime He wishes. Being quick to listen and slow to speak is a very wise policy. You cannot learn anything with your mouth moving too fast, but you glean an abundance of knowledge when you listen intently. Mature church leadership will want to make sure you are spiritually mature enough to do what the calling will demand of you. However, church leadership members are only humans, and they are not the one God is calling to go out on the mission field. Because of this, they may not feel the same way about things as you will. We had this happen on our first calling and had to go through some very lengthy testing of things and through prayerful waiting on the Holy Spirit for us to to determine if the calling was of God.

Matthew 6:24 tells us, "No man can serve two masters: for either he will hate the one, and love the other; or else he will hold to the one, and despise the other. You cannot serve God and mammon."

Let's look at some other meanings of this passage and see if we can get a better understanding of its different applications. Granted, you cannot serve both God and mammon—or walk in the world and in the Spirit. You must have your hand in God's hand, being led by Him. Therefore, when man comes up against what God has planned, a final decision must be made, which must be pleasing to God. Leadership may still say no, and that does not always mean that their answer was not spiritually discerned to the best of their abilities. It may be that you are called but the timing of implementing the calling is yet future. Therefore, if your heart is still ringing out loud and clear with the desire to go, go right back to God and give Him full control to bring you a clearer answer. God is in control and will with time clarify His desire for you, so slow down and wait. With time and prayer come clearer answers. Christ had many leaders in opposition to His mission from the Father, and so can you. Just make sure it is not your desires running wild and getting in the way of hearing God correctly.

Please do not automatically think that because church leadership says no, it is not from God, or that they are not listening to God as much as you are. They are church leaders because their hearts are filled with doing a ministry that is pleasing to God, and they will have your best interest at heart. We must remember that no one can or should try to place God in his or her tiny little box when God's ways are higher than ours and His desires and will are always for the betterment of all mankind. No man, not one, will ever know the full will of God upon another man's life, let alone upon his own.

Chapter 23

How to Prepare for a Mission Outreach

Begin by serving anywhere you can in the local body

GOD HAS MADE it clear in His Word that we must love one another.

> Beloved, let us love one another, for love comes from God, and everyone who loves is born of God and knows God.
>
> —1 John 4:7-8

This love underlies our service in the kingdom of God. You can say you love God, but if you do not have a servant heart filled with unselfish love for others, you will not be serving anyone but yourself for selfish gain.

The person God uses will have a track record of serving anywhere he can. This is just natural to servants. They receive a joy inside that rises to overflowing when other people's needs are being met. How can God use you when you do not have any desire to unselfishly help others? Sure, it's easy to do once in a while, especially when it is not going to take you very long. However, a real servant does not care about the length of time it will take or the hardship it may cause him. What matters is that people's needs are being fully met.

Let me share a little of what God placed in my path over the years as part of my training in becoming a missionary. From the time I became a Christian, I found myself frequently involved in assisting around the church. Some days it was planting grass or trees, laying a sidewalk, painting a prop for the kids' play, ushering, vacuuming the carpets, and on and on. I did not have very much Bible knowledge then, so I could not help in the more mature areas. The thing I remember about those days was that I was having fun doing it, and it didn't feel like a burden to me, but a new type of joy in my heart that left me feeling fulfilled inside. Before I was a Christian, I spent most of my time destroying people's lives and marriages through my sinful lifestyle. But now it felt so different to experience building up and encouraging people in the Lord. I believe servanthood is one of God's gifts to the body of Christ that He gives to teach the body to express godly love toward one another through serving each other.

God is always busy training us through ways we may never even notice. Yet we will still grow in our abilities to serve unselfishly in meeting the needs of others. When you are busy serving in any capacity, what you are doing for others is developing new knowledge and abilities in you. To lead and guide a church becomes much easier when you have experienced the different levels of needs you will face, both small and great. Servant leadership ensures proper functioning and continued unity in a body.

On the other hand, when you aim in the dark, you miss the target more than you hit it. God knows far better than we what it takes to keep a body growing and loving from within itself. He does this so we will reach out and show the world the difference between being a Christian and living in the world with all its selfish ways. We will never reach many in the world if we cannot show them the difference between their world and ours.

Why did you personally become a Christian? Was it because you saw a real difference in Christian lives and found yourself desiring to have the peace and hope expressed by the way they lived their lives? Was it because you just wanted to make new friends, do new things, and could leave when you did not like it any longer? I am sure you fit in the first category or you would not even be reading this book.

Praying for one another is another way God is training His body to care about others and their needs. James 5:13-16, Ephesians 6:18, Philippians 4:6, and Acts 1:14 speak of prayer as one of the most important parts of a Christian's growth. Yet prayer is one of the most neglected areas of many of our lives and is the main reason we all struggle so much with sin and temptations. When we serve others with unselfish prayer, we often get to see God answering those prayers. When others pray in return for our needs and spiritual walk, we get to enjoy a new-found spiritual strength in our lives with Christ.

Maturing as a Christian should automatically cause you to grow as a servant. People will ask you to explain biblical things to them or seek guidance for their weaknesses or ask how to grow as a Christian. The Lord always uses our own growth to serve other people's needs. If you have gained a position without a servant's heart, it will not be long until people will no longer come to you for help or follow your advice. The reason is simple: you will have selfish motives behind what you share, and you will want some selfish recognition from what advice you gave them. The old "pat me on the back, I'm such an awesome guy, aren't I very special, you are so lucky to have me to come to for help" routine. Little gods, as I call them. They do not last long in the ministry because people quickly turn from them.

You cannot be an effective missionary without an unselfish servant heart and life. Ask your church leaders for more opportunities to serve in the body and watch them glow at your request. They are always looking for members in the body whom they can see truly love the Lord and want to express their love by serving like Christ did. Missions need servant-hearted people, who are few and far between. Mission work is often held back because of this issue.

A team of servants busy getting someone's special needs taken care of is a beautiful thing to watch. Their joy explodes when they see their efforts blessing someone's life, and hope radiates from their faces as they look at each other in awe of what God has just done for them. The reward for serving others cannot be measured by earthly standards because it comes to you from on high, from God's own hand, full of blessings overflowing on your life. Be sure you are a continuous good servant or else do not even think of becoming a missionary.

Get more training in Scripture and in your leadership abilities

No one can ever be trained enough to handle everything you may face in life. Gaining knowledge is an ongoing experience that helps make our lives somewhat understandable. Knowledge comes from seeking correct information. Understanding comes from the experience of life's successes and failures in trying to apply that knowledge. Wisdom is knowing what you must do the next time when a particular situation arises. You are only as wise as you know what to do. Therefore, if you honestly evaluate your knowledge and abilities and seek to add strength to those weak areas, you will become a useful tool, accomplishing much. Failing to properly evaluate your abilities is foolish, and being foolish is a major topic that Proverbs instructs us to avoid.

When the people you are serving come to you for answers and you give them an uneducated answer that fails them, you have lost your witness and their trust in you. At times we failed in knowing what to say to people—or having the right answers—and people simply refused to accept what we tried to give them as help. You will be useless to most people if you are not what they expect you to be. Remember, God is not a God of confusion, but of order and stability. God may give you the calling, but you must get yourself prepared to be the best you can be by having your spiritual toolbox packed to overflowing. When you are going on vacation across the country, you do not just run out and jump in the car empty-handed and take off. You sit down, look at the needs you will have for the trip, and then pack enough clothes and other items to meet those needs. You must figure the cost of food, gas, shelter, and any possible breakdowns. You make sure you have enough medicine that might be needed. You plan sight-seeing areas along the way to keep things interesting and exciting. You get advice from someone when you are not sure which is the best way to go or the best places to eat or anything else. Why? Because when you know what lies ahead, you are not caught off guard, come up short, or fail to reach your goal.

There is little worse than people who get lost or thoroughly confused, and everyone begins yelling and blaming each other. There are far more failures each day due to poor planning or not being properly equipped, than there are successes due to good planning. Some people jump in over their heads into deep water when they do not know how to swim yet and drown themselves. Being properly trained in the areas you anticipate needing help with beforehand will give you a great edge in succeeding in the long run.

Your church leadership is there to help you evaluate your abilities and measure you up to the calling. Follow their advice, especially when you can see clearly that you are not measuring up as you should. Sometimes it will take not just months, but years to get your act together enough to go meet the challenge ahead of you.

Get others involved in your calling

Whenever the Lord decides to put a long-term mission together, He also puts a long- term mission team together to support that calling. He also gives you some very intricate details that must be in place before He sends you out. Believe me, we had many intricate details to take care of each time we went out. It is not easy to recognize them, so slow down and keep waiting on the Lord to show them to you.

When you are putting a large support team together, many different positions must be filled. First, you need a very well-qualified and mature team leader. Without him or her, there will be constant chaos and bickering. This person will be responsible to see that you are kept alive in the minds of those who are your supporters, no matter what way they are connected. That person will need someone to take care of the newsletters you will be sending home monthly to be copied to everyone on your support mailing list. The supporter mailing list consists of helpers, prayer warriors, and financial supporters. Also needed will be someone who can handle the finances and see that they are properly recorded and that you receive your monthly support abroad on time. This person will bring the whole team together often for a special time of prayer for you. There is no way just one or two people can handle such a large amount of work. They will burn out and become dissatisfied and fall to the wayside just when you need them the most. So take time and put together a minimum of five people on your team. There will be those who, for one reason or another, need to step down, need extra help, go on vacation, or get sick, so have others trained to step in and fill the vacancies.

God gave us wisdom from His Word about doing things alone. He did not intend man to be alone—that is why He brought Adam a beautiful helpmate in Eve. Try populating the world by yourself—you can't. Then there was Moses, who complained that he could not speak clearly, so God placed Aaron by his side to give him some added strength. Good old Noah had sons to help him build the ark. The feeding of the widows and orphans in the book of Acts was handled by a team of seven godly men.

Christ Himself chose not to do His ministry alone and chose twelve men from varied walks of life to come alongside Him to spread the gospel message. You can see that Scripture is not lacking in events where a team of co-workers were put together to perform God's work.

Please be wrapped in a well-staffed team and feel the strength that flows from it through the entire duration of your calling. Look at it this way: if your house is burning, are you going to just grab the garden hose and say, "I can put it out all by myself?" Are you not going to run to the phone and call the firemen? One way, you will lose the battle for sure; the other way, they will win their battle with numbers and greater ability. The choice, my friend, is yours. Be wise—be a winner.

You cannot just reach out quickly and grab people from just those you know and, bingo, you have your support team. Nothing could be further from the truth. This type of good-old-buddy effort will end up with you becoming very disappointed. This is the time to slow down and be extremely careful whom you choose for any of the positions. You must be the one to choose the leader of your team. Choose someone who is very like-minded with you, both in goals and intentions. Make sure you allow God to confirm each person being added. Spend time in prayer and talking to church leadership about each person before you actually add him or her to your team. A long-term commitment is not easy for some people to stick to. Many fall away at the first sign of it being too hard for them, or they find a new financial problem at home that will not allow them to continue any longer.

When someone has spent hours before God seeking His will, God will place on his or her heart such a burning desire to make sure you succeed that it truly becomes that person's calling as well. And remember, the calling belongs to all of you. That is why it is called a team. If people fall away from the team while you are out on the field, you cannot just run home and throw a new team together. This is why you need to take your time now and do it right the first time. You are the steward of not just the money God gives you, but also of everything God gives you, including the calling, the team, and the work.

Gathering your team

First: Here is a good suggestion given to us near our beginning as missionaries. Start from within your own circle of friends and work outwards.

A little warning here: even Christ was not received in His own home town while he was growing up, and you be rejected at times as well. People in general are afraid of commitments, especially if they are long-term. Some of these friends won't even say anything about your calling, so do not get depressed. They also could be afraid that you may ask them to be a part of it and they do not know how to tell you they do not want to be a part of it. So watch the body language and do not press things upon people. Remember, the best and proper way to ask them is for them to pray for you and your gathering of a team; then leave it to God to call out His team and supporters.

Second: Start visiting the different groups at your church—the home kinships (fellowships), Bible studies, men's groups, and women's groups. I'm sure you can think of your own list. Ask if they will allow you to come share your vision, but do not pressure anyone, ever. If it is of God, He will open the door.

Third: When someone comes up to you and begins asking strong informative questions about your calling, you can rest assured God has prompted him or her to check out a desire He has placed on his or her heart. Always give thorough answers. The questions usually go like this: How do you know God is calling you? How long have you been a Christian? Have you taken time to study the culture, political issues, cost, and dangers there? His list may be long, but show him that he is important to you and you appreciate his coming to find answers to his questions. Assure him he can call you if he has other questions later. Remember, he might be making a decision to be a part of the calling. Should he come later and say he believes God is telling him to become a part, God will give you a peace inside to confirm that it is of Him, or He will give a check in your spirit if it is not of Him. I cannot emphasize this enough. Slow down and pray about all the decisions you are making. God will never fail to reveal His will if we do not get in the way.

We ended up with over three hundred people stateside belonging to our calling in some way or the other, and almost all of them stayed faithful through the calling from beginning to end. They were as much a part of the calling as we were, and they knew it. We made sure to mention the importance of their participation often because that is how we really felt about each of them.

Once Sunny and I were at a home fellowship just before our third calling where we knew only a few people. We had been asked to come share what we believed God was calling us to go and do. Afterwards, two men came up and asked all the right questions and we did our best to answer them correctly. When we finished answering all their questions, they said they wished to take it all before the Lord for a few days and would get back with us about being a part of meeting our needs. We felt we had known them for a long time because we were so at peace with each of them. About two weeks went by and they both called. Each one believed God was telling him to become part of our support team in any way we needed him to be. We met with each a few more times and then made a decision to bring both of them on board.

One of the men, Kerry, went on to become our team leader for about five years. God used Kerry to bring on board a bookkeeper named John, someone to handle the newsletters, and people to handle many other areas and needs. By the time he was finished, he had people in all the areas needed to serve this calling. God had used him mightily to put together a very strong team, and the team did not waste any time in getting to work as they began visiting other groups and sharing what this calling was about and all its needs. They did yard sales, helped purchase a 20'x8' shipping container, and worked at getting it packed right.

Calvary Chapel had us speak to the body a few times about the calling and what we hoped to accomplish in Uganda. Before we knew it, we had over three hundred people as part of our general support team. Many were prayer warriors, while some were doing both prayer and financial support. Both are important to any calling, as you cannot have one without the other.

When we were really close to our departure date, Kerry and the main team put together one great going away party. There were too many people to count, and we got hugs and kisses from them all, so much so that it took weeks to get the wrinkles out of our lips. We also gained more supporters that night, still without ever asking for money even once. Sunny looked at me, I looked at Sunny, and we wondered what God was up to in bringing so many people into this calling. Having this many people was making us just a little scared of the unknown on the one hand, and extremely excited on the other. These kinds of unknown things are why it is so important to let God do His thing. When you or I do it, we are in the dark as to what is going to be needed and fall way short of meeting the needs set before us. But God, being the all knowing God He is, has it all in His hands and will see to it that it is done with or without us. Nothing can quench what is of God. Maybe it can be slowed down a little, but God is faithful to complete the good work He has begun.

Getting your finances in order

Finances can make or break a mission. You must handle them correctly right from the start. Being a good steward is the only thing God will accept when handling anything He gives you to take care of. If you lack the abilities to keep good bookkeeping records, get someone else involved who does know how. Pride comes before the fall, so humble yourself and admit where you are weak. Your gift may be somewhat different from the next person's, but all can work together for the same cause and accomplish it much easier and without as many errors. Read the story about the parable of the talents in Matthew 25:14-30.

When you read part one of this book, you saw firsthand how well God provides when you are being very careful to correctly handle all He gives you. Worrying about receiving enough money has no place in the mind of a missionary who has truly been sent by God. Matthew 6:25-34 tells us never to worry about earthly things since God will provide for them if we really need them. We should always be careful not to let our fleshly desires get in the way of what God wants us to do with His funding and supplies. God explains this in Matthew 6:19-24, about how we cannot serve both God and mammon (money, or treasures of this world).

One of the saddest things, told to me by a city official in Mbale, Uganda, was: "Pastor Jay, please do not be like so many of the other missionaries who seem to come and build a small church, and then build themselves a nice big house to live like a king, and then forget my people's suffering."

This statement has never left my mind for a moment in any of my decisions since then. Sadly, most missions operate on the rate of 75 percent for in-house needs and 25 percent for meeting the needs of others. We have always operated with 80 percent for the needs God makes known to us and 20 percent for the in-house needs. The thing about it, though, is that we grew faster, met more needs, saved more souls, and still never asked anyone for money. Our personal needs and the needs around us were met by God to the max. He never failed to provide for us or for the needs.

The other part of your finances that you must not leave unfinished is your own personal debts at home. By this I mean what you owe before you are called out. You cannot take these debts with you and then think you can use mission money to pay them off. You must get your house in order first by paying them off with your own abilities and through the income you have generated through your own labor. Understand this, when people are donating to the work God has called you to and they hear that you are paying off old personal debts, you will lose them faster than you can blink an eye. People are getting involved with your calling because they feel led to assist the work and the people where you are going to serve, not for you to line your own pockets with.

You will send home newsletters in which your team will share with your supporters what is being accomplished since the last newsletter went out. From these newsletters, people can pretty well judge what you are doing and accomplishing with the funds you are receiving. You must have good records of all you are spending, so that if anyone wishes to see what you have done with these funds, you can quickly show them without any fear of misuse. So go out without any debts left behind and go out unhindered in the work you have been called to do.

By doing it the right way, you will see how abundantly God can and will provide for you. Luke 6:38 says, "Give and it will be given unto you over flowing into your lap." God will give it to you as much as you actually need, but He can take it away just as fast as He has given it to you if you abuse His gifts. So please make sure you get the help you need to start out on the right foot so you don't come limping home later because of failure.

Finances should not be worried about. Discipline them as God would expect of you, and you will not go without your needs being met. Please *do not ever* solicit for money for any reason. Give people the full information about the need but absolutely no solicitation for the funding of the need. Remember this and do not forget it: what God has called together, He will also provide all the supplies for—all of it, all the time, without fail. When you yourself ask for money, you are stealing God's glory from Him, and you will end up not knowing for sure if it was really of Him for you to go in the first place.

You can reasonably assure yourself that you are in His will when you let God handle all the details and the funding. Your job is to do the work that comes with it and ensure that it is to His glory. As I have said before, part one of this book should help remove any doubt of God's ability to take care of His calling through you. It has nothing to do with your abilities, but it does have to do with your servant heart attitude. Focus on completing the work placed in your hand by God.

This information is hard for some people to adjust to, but you must adjust to it. From the time we are little, we run up to mom or dad and ask for money. It is our habit to ask for money, but even our parents received their money by doing the work asked of them. The person above them then made sure they were paid for their hard efforts. God is no different in rewarding the work we do for His company/ministry that collects and feeds lost souls. So what do you do about it? How do you go about doing it right?

First: Do not solicit for funds; just issue full information, ask for prayer, and then trust in God to provide.

Second: Know all the details that will be needed to fulfill your calling. Such details include the monthly cost figures for housing (be it renting or buying), food, clothing, shipping, airline tickets (one-way or round-trip), vehicle, study materials, building costs, government paperwork fees, and whatever else you can find out that might be needed. You should then get with your team and put your heads together and make out a well-thought-out list of things for people to be praying over. When the list is ready, insert it into a newsletter. To keep the long list from scaring some of the readers to death, thinking they have to try and meet everything on the list, add this note for them and just say:

> God may only ask you to be a small part of this calling by just taking on one small area to help us with. God may ask you to take on a larger portion. It does not matter. What really matters to God is that you are listening to Him and are willing to do what you can for His glory and for other people's needs.

Again, I will say it: absolutely no solicitation, just full information, and ask for prayer only.

Here is another example that you read about in part one of God meeting all your needs if it is of Him. We were asked by the government of Uganda to come alongside them and help meet the needs of a refugee camp deep in rebel-held territory near the Sudan border. The other missions refused to go because of the high danger level from the rebels. We had never ministered in a refugee camp before and needed some serious help from those in the know. We went to prayer, seeking God's will on it. God did confirm, with the needs of that camp growing louder and louder, pounding away in our hearts, just how many people were starving to death, had little to no water (and that was contaminated water), and no medical supplies or treatment available. After performing much investigation with those in the know, we found that the dollar amount would be large to set everything up. We'd never had that kind of financial need before. I sent the full information to our home church for the body to lift in prayer. Within a few days, Samaritan's Purse, a large relief mission organization, donated $10,000 toward the medicine, and they gave us thirty 20'x100' blue tarps to cover a makeshift field hospital. They also sent three large truckloads of relief food supplies to the camp immediately. By the second week, our home church told us we received over $18,000 in a special offering to help meet the needs. They did not know the full cost as we did not know what would be needed, just the need. God in His mightiness met every penny of that need; the people there were blessed abundantly. Again I say, He never gives you something to do for Him and then falls short of doing it.

Sometimes we hear people asking for specific amounts of money, like "if everyone gave $20 or $100, we can get the job done." Again I say to you, it is not we who get it done. If it is of the Lord, it will be the Lord Who will get it done. If you ask people for too much money, those with little cannot be a part of it. If you ask for too little, those who could have given much more do not. Please leave the business of raising money to God, not you. Just ask for prayer; then sit back and watch God do His wonderful thing. God has never failed to meet our needs at any time, for any reason, ever. When God brings your funding, He gets the glory, and you will be doing it for Him through His great power and love.

Making sure you are healthy enough to go

Just like your own personal debts have no business being a part of your calling, neither do your prior health issues if they are going to be a burden placed on the mission to pay for those medical needs. If an illness comes upon you after you are out, then it should be the responsibility of your supporters to meet. If it is serious, then you should consider returning home for long-term care.

People are supporting the work you are sent to do, not the personal issues you carry along as extra baggage. If you do have an existing medical problem, and it is being taken care of by some other financial way and not from your monthly support, then it might be okay. The reason I say it might be okay is that if it becomes a bigger problem than you have private finances to cover, you must consider returning home. This is not a dogmatic statement, as God may want one or more of your supporters to step up and meet the cost of the care. I suggest this to you: be honest about all your needs, be they health issues or support; do this right in the beginning. Then wait on God to see if God moves upon anyone to meet that need. Again I say, do not ask for money at any time. Just share honestly and openly with everyone the full details about your calling. This includes your health and financial needs.

Please do not go out if you know you have health issues that would become a burden on the other missionaries you would be serving with. Here is a good example: Sunny and I had made friends with a very elderly lady from England who had come to Uganda to do a ministry pretty much on her own desires. I will call her Mary to protect her identity. She had medical needs that kept growing from month to month, and she needed to come to our house to get some much-needed rest. She worked in a small town a little north of us and would barely make it to our house before dropping from exhaustion. Sunny nursed her back to health each time she came until she was well enough to go back to her ministry. Granted, her heart was in the right place, wanting to serve the needs of others, but she was becoming a serious burden to all the other missionaries in the area since she also went to them for many of her other needs. She seemed to never have enough money to meet her needs and went around begging for handouts from the local business stores and the mission community. We all felt sorry for her and tried hard to help her when we could. Her way of going about things was making the local people very sour toward her, and they asked us to tell her to return home. It was becoming a sore spot with many of the other missionaries, who believed as we did that she should return to England because she was around eighty years old and had little support to live on, let alone to support her ministry.

One day she had a mini-stroke in a local taxi and they brought her to our house since they knew we knew her. Sunny nursed her back to a traveling health status, and then we told her she needed to go home and get well before thinking of coming back. We also went a step further and stated she had blown her Christian witness by begging for financial help from the local businesses. We also explained that if God was not the one supporting her calling, it was more than likely not His calling, because if it was of Him, He would provide for the needs of that calling. At this she became angry, but she did go home and did not come back out.

God is not poor, and He does provide abundantly for what He has called into existence and protects from failure. This is another proof of when something is of God. He will supply for it. If it is not of Him, you will constantly have to beg for money, just like many of the TV evangelists do.

Please make sure you are not going to be a burden on your supporters because of some pre-existing medical condition. Nor should you go and become a burden on the mission or local community in that area. Go out when you know you should go out, when God has provided for it without any question of where the provision came from or what it is going to be used for.

Your household cannot be divided

This section deals with the importance of unity among married couples and their primary obligation to their dependent children. God will not call one of you out long-term to serve without calling your spouse to come alongside you. Luke 11:17 clearly tells us "that a house divided against itself will fall," meaning that it would be destroyed. God would never divide a Christian household for any reason, as it can open the door for many kinds of temptations to creep in and cause division.

Should you take your dependent children with you on the mission field? Children are the responsibility of the parents who gave them birth.

The children's needs have the highest priority in your overall decision to go to the mission field. Make sure what you feel called by God to do is really of Him. This cannot be expressed highly enough, as it is of great importance to your family and how your children may feel about Christ down the line. If you abandon them or leave them carelessly for what you feel led to do, you will send a message to them that they are not very important to you. So take the time to talk at length with your children, making sure they truly understand what and why you are feeling led to go serve.

Never go out on a long-term mission outreach and leave your children behind; the repercussions could be disastrous. If you cannot take them with you, stay at home. Remember, you do not have to go out to be part of a mission outreach. The teams at home keep the missionaries out there working and supported. Just join in and serve from where they need you, with your arms around their every need. Kids need you there by them.

I know from experience that no mission stands a chance of accomplishing much unless it has a strong support team at home encouraging its missionaries on through their many trials and tribulations. Many people make the mistake of thinking that God is calling them out on the field as a missionary, when He just wants to use the gifts He has given them to serve a foreign calling right from their own home. Each is as important as the other, as both callings are from God. We just need to be obedient and do it for God's glory, not ours.

Chapter 24

Can God Use me at my Level of Spiritual Growth?

A newer Christian's role

BEING A NEW Christian is always a blessing to those who have been around for a good while. New Christians have an on-fire fresh zeal that excites others, and it helps to rekindle dying flames. Having things come at you daily the same way day after day can take away some of the joy of what needs to be done. God, being the all knowing God He is, knows we need to have our spiritual batteries recharged from time to time.

When a seasoned missionary has been out there year after year, the mud hut becomes a mud hut, poverty is just poverty, and after a while you become sort of numb to the things going on around you. Seeing this, God sends out an on-fire, highly-motivated, highly-excited, ready-for-anything new believer; this helps you to see clearly again all the work He has been accomplishing through your hard efforts for His glory. I personally know that I got numb to things from time to time; I needed new people to come out to reopen my eyes again to what God was doing through our mission efforts. When they did this, we would find new joy and excitement about the work that was there for us each new day.

New Christians can be used powerfully by God to assist the work, but they cannot do the work that a more mature Christian can do. Simply put, a new Christian knows he or she cannot present the message on Sunday morning, nor share it very well on the field, until his or her training is more complete.

The intermediate Christian's role

This group of Christians performs a lot of the helps-type work in keeping a mission running as it should each day. They know Scripture well enough to help in group studies, in youth groups, orphan programs, and many of the administrative needs that must be performed daily. They are limited only by the amount of Scripture they actually know. Being honest about how much you really know will save you a lot of embarrassment down the line.

We had a young man in his early twenties who served our mission really well in areas that he had enough knowledge and maturity for. This is to be expected and is a part of growing as a Christian, and it should not be looked down on at all. He has since matured even more and is performing in additional mature roles for the mission.

The more mature Christian's role

Leadership is always placed in the hands of the more mature since they have the experience and knowledge to get the job done as God would expect. The books of Timothy and Titus contain the qualifications of these types of leaders, and mature Christians should match up to those qualifications.

Thinking more highly of yourself than you should always creates more problems than usable answers. If you are not sure of your maturity, ask your church leadership what they believe your abilities for a leadership position are according to their knowledge of you.

When you are on the mission field, the decisions you make can be a blessing to the mission; on the other hand, they can bring failure and even danger upon everyone serving with you. When God sees you have enough leadership abilities to fulfill the needs of the calling, He can and will use you in many different ways.

I was asked to be the chief warden for the US Embassy in Uganda for the district around Jinja. This meant I was to look after all the American citizens who lived in that district. I was also asked to be the main speaker for the US Embassy's memorial service for the 9/11 attacks. As I have said before, the Ugandan government asked me to take over the needs of a refugee camp located deep inside rebel-held territory and see that they got food, water, and medical assistance. The ways in which God can use you for His glory and for the needs of others are unlimited, and you must be ready.

First: A good leader must be in the Word, preparing daily because he will often be asked to meet a need or fill a ministry opening at the last minute.

Second: Timothy 4:2 states that we are to "preach the word; be ready in season and out of season; reprove, rebuke, exhort, with great patience and instruction." The key phrase in this verse to pay attention to is "be ready." The only way you can be ready is to have been studying His Word in depth and preparing to share your knowledge in an understandable way. When you have these in place, God can call you at any time, for any reason, and you'd better be ready to take care of His business.

This position is not for the beginner or the intermediate Christian, but only for the mature Christian with good experience under his belt. You do not go to the druggist for heart surgery; he has some knowledge, but he is limited in its use. Likewise, the partially trained Christian is limited in his usability. There are things each can do well, yet there are things neither one has any business trying to handle. The bottom line is this: the beginner and the intermediate Christian simply do not have enough spiritual tools in their spiritual tool boxes to accomplish the bigger task.

When you read about many of the different experiences Sunny and I have been through over the years in part one of this book, you saw a progression of our spiritual growth. God still used us mightily everywhere we went, from the time we first went out with fewer abilities, up through much more spiritual maturity, including training those who were to take over the work. God never gave us more than He had placed the ability in us to handle, and He will not give you too much to handle either. Do not go past your abilities and fail God, fail others, and hinder the ministry. Please just be honest with yourself and others as to what your real abilities are, both physically and spiritually. If you do this, you will do just fine, and you will love what you are doing in serving God and others.

Chapter 25

What Documents Do I Need Before Going Out?

The first requirement is an up-to-date American passport

IF YOU DO not have a passport yet, simply go to the nearest Post Office and pick up the application form, follow the instructions carefully, and send it with the required funds to the address stated in the application.

Part of the requirements is having some top quality passport photos taken. Please make sure you get no fewer than six for a short-term outreach and twelve for a long-term stay. You will be asked by most foreign government offices anywhere you go for a passport photo to be attached to the other documents they may require from you. This will be asked from you in almost every office for every action they need you to take to work in their country.

If you already have a passport and you have used it somewhat often, make sure you have new blank pages added for stamping in and out of any country because you will use them up quickly. When an officer has difficulty finding a place in your passport to stamp, you may get some unneeded and unwanted hassle. A little commonsense thinking helps offset much of these types of headaches you can encounter.

Buying one-way or round-trip airline tickets

Most of your ticket purchasing will be determined by your planned length of stay where you are headed. There is more to it, though. When you are going to go long-term, most airlines will require you to purchase round-trip tickets when you do not yet have a work permit for the country you are headed. You can get through this requirement by buying tickets in which the return portion can be refunded after your arrival there, when you get your work permit. You must have this authorization ahead of time by the airline you are to travel with, or you will not get it refunded. Almost all countries you travel to will require round-trip tickets to be in your possession before entry will be granted, unless you have a work permit stamped in your passport, which you can only get after you have been in that country for a while and your paperwork is finalized.

As you travel, you can see some of the countries you are traveling through. You can ask for a layover in any country on your way to or from your destination at an added cost. The cost is not much if you compare it to how much it would cost to come there at some later time. If you lay over, you will need to book a hotel room in advance. That can be done through a travel agency with little to no cost to you. We usually took three days at a place we had not been to before, and we found it sufficient. Sometimes the airlines have a hard time filling a flight, so they will lay you over and put you up in a hotel at their expense. We had this happen to us twice, once in Amsterdam, Holland, and another time in Rome, Italy—poor us.

Another advantage available when you are overseas working long- term is a "See America Pass" you can get when you are getting ready to come home on furlough. This is only available through American airlines and the airlines connected with them. With this pass you are only charged $100 per airport landing once you arrive in the states.

You still pay for your round-trip tickets as usual, minus the missionary discounts, but if you wish to visit other friends and family around the country, you will only have to pay $100 per airport you land at. If you have to go through a second airport to get to your next stop, you will pay a reduced rate of $75 for that extra stop.

The airlines are charged a fee every time they land at an airport, and that is then passed on to the ticket holder. You must begin using your "See America Pass" within thirty days of your arrival in the states.

Sunny and I landed in Boston and took a week to visit a grandson (cost: $100 each); then we flew to Florida to visit our oldest daughter and more grandkids (cost: $100 each); then we went to Fort Worth to see our youngest daughter and more grandkids (cost: $100 each); then we traveled to Alaska to see our eldest son through two airports (cost: $100 plus $75 each); then we flew back to Washington state to see one of my brothers (cost: $100); and finally we came into Albuquerque, New Mexico, to finish our at-home furlough (cost: $100 each). With our missionary discounted tickets, we ended up only paying $2,300 each to visit everyone, and this included our return to Uganda. The "See America Pass" is a great benefit. Try traveling to just one of those destinations, which could cost you at least $600-$1,000 for each person for each stop.

Missionary-subsidized or reduced tickets are available now through most airlines. We used Menno travel agency. You will be required to have proof that you are going to be serving as a missionary. A letter from your church can usually handle this with any airline. The letter must be on letterhead paper and placed in an address-printed envelope. Most travel agencies can now book your missionary-reduced tickets for you. If you have any problems in getting them, go on the Internet and check out each airline about their missionary policies on subsidized or discounted tickets, and you will find one that goes your way, or at least most of the way there.

Visitors visas for entering a foreign country

Some countries allow you to get your visitor's visa as you enter their country while others may require that you have one ahead of time. This usually does not apply when you are only going for a short-term stay. You can check this out on the Web. However, if you are going for the long haul, you will still need a visitor's visa to enter the country and don't even mention wishing to stay long-term. You will be held up for hours and possibly even sent back home if you talk about wanting to stay on and work there. The simple way to do this is to enter on a visitor's visa and keep getting it renewed as you work on getting a work permit.

Work permits will become mandatory in order stay there long-term. You will be required to have a good resume, your school documents for any higher education, all your transcripts, grades, and degrees obtained. If you have any special training like medical, electrical, plumbing, building, or in the educational field, you must have all of your licenses for each of them and proof of your experience. The medical fields will be much hindered in what they are allowed to do, just as a foreigner would be when coming to America. They do really need medical workers, so they will allow you to do pretty much what your records say you have the ability to do. The main thing is, make the officals, or medical staff feel like they are just as knowledgeable as you are, and work around their weaknesses as you teach or show them very gently what is right.

You may be asked to do some teaching in local school programs, depending on your skills. This should be counted as a ministry outreach and done with good long-term planning. Mission work is hardly ever just teaching the Bible; you must be able to help people meet the needs of their households when you have those skills. The great thing about this type of ministry is that it tears down closed doors that would normally be shut. Plus, you will make some much-needed friendships that will enhance your life and the mission work the whole team is out there to accomplish.

Driver's license requirements

This starts before you leave the States. You will need to get an international driver's license so you will be able to drive when you first arrive. An international driver's license can be obtained at any AAA (American Automobile Association) location. Get the form and fill it out, show them your stateside driver's license, give them the passport photos they require, the ten dollars it costs, and you are on your way.

When you are only going short-term, this is all you will need to be able to drive anywhere you are for a short time. When you are going there long-term, you must work toward getting a local driver's license soon. This is somewhat like getting a driver's license in the States. You will be made to pass a test, your vehicle must pass a very stringent vehicle check, and you must have purchased local auto insurance. Insurance can be a bit on the expensive side since drivers in foreign countries are not known to be safe drivers at all, but the insurance is a must. *Do not ever* let your insurance or driver's license expire. The penalties could be more than a couple of days in a flea- and rat-infested jail cell. Plus, the fines are heavy. You can bribe your way out of it, but you will also blow your Christian witness, and that you will not be able to buy back.

You should also keep your international driver's license up to date. You will sometimes need to cross over into a neighboring country, and it will keep you from having to pay some exorbitant fee for just a short visit. The international driver's license is good for ten years, and then you will need to renew it. Some AAA offices allow you to do it by mail, but you can just as easily get it renewed while you are home on one of your furloughs since you do not have to wait for them to run completely out to renew them. This license is also nice to have should you lay over on your trips in some country you wish to see more of than the downtown area. A little safety tip: make sure to ask what side of the road they drive on when renting a car and driving on the wrong side with everyone laughing and yelling, "Yup, just another dumb American who doesn't know his left from his right."

Police report for the last three years

Most countries require you to produce documentation from the stateside police of your past driving and arrest records. Your local vehicle department should be able to print out your last three years' driving record for you in a matter of fifteen minutes or so. The police department will need to see you personally in order to get your criminal history since it is privately-secured information. This also needs to be for the last three years. Make many copies of both, as you will need them. These are very necessary in getting your work permit in most foreign countries. So please do not forget to get them ahead of time because you cannot get them any other way but by being there personally. When you are going for a short-term outreach, you will not need these documents. But if you think there is any chance you might want to stay and continue working, get them for safety's sake. Remember, they cannot be gotten by anyone else but you in the flesh.

Shots and dental records

These documents are needed whether you are going out for a short term or a long one. Shots are required for just about every overseas visit. You can find out which shots are needed where you are going by simply getting on the Internet, going to that country's site, and asking for the shot requirements. You can also go to a travel agency and get the same information. Your doctor or a hospital can administer the shots for you. But please make sure you get proof of all shots you are taking by getting a record book from them that shows each shot you took, the dosage, the date it was administered, and the expiration date. You will be asked to show your shot record book when buying your overseas tickets, when leaving the States, when entering another country, and for work permits. So please make sure you have them and keep them in a secure place, with copies in other locations. Making many extra copies is a good idea on all your important documents. Do not put all your eggs in one basket, so to speak; place copies in several of your bags.

Dental records are more for your own needs. Some places you may go to may not have X-ray equipment, and any X-rays you carry with you may help you not lose teeth that could have been saved. They love just pulling teeth, and your money.

All medical and health records you can get will be a blessing to you, especially should something serious happen to you and you need medical attention quickly. Allergies, special medicines, and any other thing you know might be helpful for another doctor to know—bring it with you. You do not want someone having to do research about your needs when they have little or no skills and poor equipment. Go prepared to the max for the worst scenario and you won't be sorry.

Marriage license and birth certificates

A marriage license is sometimes needed when getting your work permits and for some airline tickets. The American embassy may require a marriage certificate if something as serious as a death has taken place. They do this to prove you have the right to say how the body is to be handled or where it is to be shipped.

Birth certificates are required for getting your passport, for getting foreign work permits, and for many of the other transactions required of you. Your birth certificate cannot just be copied in some copier, they must be **certified copies only,** and from your state of birth. I suggest you get a minimum of four certified copies before leaving if you are going out long-term. When you are going out short-term, you will need only one, but get two for safety's sake.

Shipping documents and manifests

When you are only going out for a short-term mission trip, you need not worry much about this. You may want to keep all the documents on your baggage in a safe place should they not show up when you do. Getting lost baggage is next to impossible without your baggage claim tickets, so protect them carefully. You might need them more than you think you will. The disappearing baggage ghost is still out there lurking to make someone miserable. Keep the baggage claim tickets in your ticket folder, and keep your ticket folder in a safe and secure place.

Sometimes you will be go on a very long-term mission trip, and the people you are going to serve with will need you to send out a shipping container. By shipping container, I mean a 20'x8', or 40'x80' metal seagoing shipping container. They can be purchased used in about any major city in the States. Make sure there is no way any type of rain will leak in on the goods, and that it is in good enough shape to pass a shipping company's inspection. Also, they must have all the manufacturing plates on them, just like a car does for its serial numbers. The next thing that is very important about the container is how you go about loading it. Please do not just throw things in as they arrive and not write them down.

You must make sure to list everything that goes into the container, in the exact place it is located. You must have a floor diagram showing where everything is actually located. The manifest of what is being shipped will be required by the customs authorities when going, and when it arrives at its destination. Everything must be in order, or you may end up waiting for months before getting your container cleared through customs. They also charge you by the day while it is being stored, and you must pay the bill or you will lose all that is inside it. Please read this again before you load a container.

You also cannot ship any type of medicine in them, unless you have prior approval from the country medical officials you are shipping to, and you must have that documentation from them to prove you have permission to bring the medicine in. Do not take this lightly because you can and will be arrested for not having them and/or face a heavy fine on top of it. You will also stand the chance of losing everything else you shipped because of it. This will cause you to lose a lot of donated money unnecessarily. Take it easy and go slowly when shipping your luggage or a container because they are important to your work.

Your luggage will be taken to customs at the airport when you arrive, and you must be able to tell them what is in each bag. When you hesitate even the slightest bit, you will be made to open them up for a deeper inspection. They can charge you customs on items in your bags if they wish, so please do not cause any delays for them while checking your baggage. Even when you have your act together, they can still shoot for a bribe from you by having you open one or more of your bags. Please do not panic; just explain to them that it is your personal stuff and that it is not for resale. Should they keep pushing you for anything further, remind them that you are just a missionary there to help the people of their country, and you are not there to take away their livelihood. Do not say this if you do not have a work permit; just say you're visiting as a missionary.

Another warning: please do not ever sound tough or act like you are trying to overpower them. Be gentle and polite, no matter how bad things may seem to be, or you will reap what you sow to the max. Water always cools down a fire, and we are supposed to be sharing and showing others we are filled with living water. When they show any kind of softness towards you, quickly thank them with sincerity. Never ever give in to a bribe, as you just make it harder on the other missionaries trying to get their baggage through and you will have blown your Christian witness.

More about shipping your baggage. You can take up to six extra bags per ticket by sending them on your flight as air cargo. That will usually cost you somewhere around $138 per bag. Before you think that is too high, you need to know that things where you are going are few and far between. Some items there are imported and are extremely expensive. A simple push mower (imported) can cost a whopping $275. Buy one and take it all apart and place different pieces in each of the trunks. You can place a lot more high cost items in there as well, and the cost will seem like nothing compared to the savings you gain by doing this. The reason for taking them apart is when the customs agent asks you what this is for, you will answer that "It's a part for my lawn mower" and because they do not see the whole thing, they will let it go on by. You must watch carefully the weight in each trunk. The airlines are extremely strict on how much each one is allowed to weigh. Whatever you do, do not go over that limit, as the extra pound cost is like triple your original figure. All you have to do is call the airline's shipping department and then follow their directions, and it will be easy for you. You do not have to call them if you are only taking the two bags everyone is allowed, but only if you need to send more baggage by air cargo. This must be at least two weeks ahead of time so they can reserve the space for them.

Getting free donations of clothes and equipment

There are free goods out there if you know where to find them, or better yet, if you are not afraid to ask the right questions. I was told by someone that silk screening shops in the United States that print clothing and such sometimes make mistakes in an order and cannot then deliver or resell them. But if you will go to them explaining you are a missionary needing clothing for the needy and you can issue them a donation certificate from your church (but only for the actual cost, not the retail cost, and pre-cleared with church leadership), you will find that they will come alongside your mission work since you are taking the goods out of the country to give away to needy people. You are not going to try to sell the items in the states, which would cause them and you serious legal problems.

The same thing can be done for equipment. Equipment can get damaged, scratched, or stained in shipment or on display and cannot be sold. The same type of donation certificate from your church for its wholesale cost can be issued, and you have some free equipment given to you via the Lord's church. Just be very polite; do not beg and do not get picky. Most dealers will find that you are bailing them out of a total loss and will assist you as much as possible.

Recommendation letters

Letters from your state congressman/woman are a good thing to have. They will give you one if you go by their local office and ask the secretary for one. Please make sure you go to the one for which you have a voter's registration card for his or her party. Tell him or her you want permission to put it in your newsletter to your supporters, expressing the help they were to your need. This will go a long way in getting their cooperation quickly. All politicians like to think they may gain a few more voters on their side of the fence, and they probably will.

Employer recommendation letters should be easier to get and will back up your job documents. Getting letters from friends and family are fine as well. Make sure you get letters from your pastoral staff at your church. Ask them all to put them on letterhead stationery. If you are going to an established mission, have that mission write letters of recommendation as well. The more recommendation letters you have, the easier it will be for you to get your work permit. Remember my warning here that you cannot do any type of work before you are in possession of your work permit. Remember, protect your witness because you are there as Christ's ambassador. Be a good one, or else don't go.

Permits and licensing

Going out on a foreign field is no different from a foreigner trying to enter America. There is processing that must be done before your arrival date. Each country has its own set of regulations and paperwork that you must submit ahead of time. While you are still in America, you can contact the embassy of the country you wish to serve in. A local federal office should be able to provide you with their physical and/or e-mail address.

The first step is to write and ask for the details and requirements for "visiting" their country. I strongly suggest you do not say up front that you want a work permit or that you wish to stay long-term. After you enter the country, you can keep renewing your visitor's visa until you have a work permit and/or a license to do business there. An NGO (non-governmental organization) license/permit is necessary even if you are only doing church work and not doing anything for profit. Remember that most governments want your money anyway they can get it, so you will find that you will need licenses for just about all you do in each district or city you do ministry in.

This is important: you will not be licensed overnight for any type of work you might need to do. We went more than a year in getting our NGO licensing and it took a few hundred dollars on top of that. You will need to hire a good local lawyer who deals with your needs. Then you will more than likely do most of the legwork. You should have an advantage that we did not have: the phones should be working now, plus cell phones and e-mail are everywhere to help get you started quicker. When we started, we had to mail everything home, and it took two weeks or more to get there and another three weeks to get back. The reason it took more time coming back is that the workers in the post offices are never in a hurry. Never have anyone send you something of any value through the mail or in a package; it will not make it to you. They will steal it no matter what it is or how valuable it is, and it will disappear.

What Documents Do I Need Before Going Out?

Second, without a visitor's visa in your possession, you will be made to pay some inflated fees to obtain one, although you can just wait and get one when you arrive. If you have one stamped in your passport, you will just line up at the proper window and be checked straight on through. Do not think you can play the tough guy with them and get by with it; that is what some tourists do and they end up suffering greatly in even higher fees, all because their attitude was bad. Show love and patience, and they will bend your way when you show them proper respect.

The post office will want copies of most of your documents. You still lose mail. They lock your box even though you are paid a year in advance. Another thing about the post office is how difficult it is to claim a package that has arrived. You have to go to the customs department and pick one of their agents, haul him back to the post office, then he will take his time opening and checking the package, hoping you will slip him a bribe.

Here is a funny but true story I pulled on one of these agents who was giving me a really bad time. My daughter, Sam, had sent me a package from Knott's Berry Farm in California, but she made the mistake of sending it surface mail, which took fourteen months in a hot hole on some slow-moving ship. When we opened it, I could see that the large sausage in it had become very rotten. The package it was in was swollen up like a balloon that was ready to burst. The guy was trying hard to get a bribe, when an idea came into my mind: I reached over, picked up the swollen sausage and my penknife, stretched out my hand in his direction and very near his face, and poked the end nearest him. The smell that came rushing out into his face was sickening, and he quickly leaned back and yelled, "You eat this junk!" At that he quickly signed off on the package, got up, and said he would rather walk back than be near that smell. Afterward, the postal clerk and I had a good time laughing, as it was pretty funny. These are the types of issues that will test you daily. If you do not blow up over them, you will gain some much-needed ground for your mission.

Most third world countries will not let you own land as a non-citizen. Uganda was very strict about our not being able to own land inside the city. Yet deep in the villages, land can be purchased from private land owners. It is a good idea to get all of the seller's relatives and neighbors to sign off on the deal in order to make sure it was actually his to sell. Getting land holdings inside the cities is only done through a leasing process. We got about an acre and a half for around $75 a year by lease, renewable in twenty years only if we showed building progress, for another twenty, than we would own it. Sunny and I, after staying in Uganda for over ten years, were issued permanent life residency. This means we are now counted just like Ugandan citizens, and we do not need a work permit any longer. This information is stamped in our passports, and it has no expiration date. We are free to come and go into Uganda any time we wish, and pay no fees as a foreigner would. It is sort of like having dual citizenship.

We also needed to get licenses for purchasing medicine for our little clinic we built in the northern part of Uganda. With a license, I could buy any type of medicine I wanted wholesale and in any amounts we needed. Medicine in a third world country is very cheap compared to the States. We could buy a bottle of 1,000 valium pills for about $15. We also bought medicine for other missionaries when they needed it through our license. Missionaries work together to help one another, as each has the ability.

The permit to have electricity is one of the hardest to obtain because the process is filled with much confusion and corruption. No one person seemed to know what he or she was doing. The biggest problem was when it came to being billed. They could mess up a bill so badly that they would have you owing hundreds of dollars, and when you showed them their mistake, it would still be there for the next six months or more. The upper officials were very corrupt, stealing funds and then placing it on other public peoples bills to pay. The public would protest the over billing, but it would take up to six months to get it corrected.

Water, phone, and building permits were all about the same. You just had to grin and bear the frustration until the process was completed. We were so used to it that we just planned around it and then counted our blessings when things came together.

We also had to get permits to work in the prison system. You had to do more than just teach the Bible—you had to have some kind of health, education, or fund-raising projects to get in the door. Then they checked up on you often to see if you were doing what you said you would. We helped with their need for medicine, clothing, and a seed program which involved very high-yield crops. The prisoners were only getting a bowl of ground porridge twice a day when we started. However, with the large amount of vegetables they were growing by using the high-yield seeds, they got more balanced meals and were much healthier and happier.

I am sure there are many other permits or licenses that you will be faced with in your calling. If you apply some of what you have read here, you should manage very well and have some hair left on your head at the end of the day. Our prayers are with you, and we hope you will have it a bit easier than we did. Greed is greed, no matter where you find it; it will be there to bite you. Review often, as it will help eliminate some of these headaches.

Chapter 26

What to do When you First Get There

Take your time, observe, and learn

WE MUST FIRST face the fact that this is not some vacation spot where we can just jump out and then go running wild, grabbing in all the sights as fast as we can. What is common to you in America may not be acceptable in the country where you are serving. Remember that trying to undo a mistake may take a long time, especially if you have insulted someone's culture. Try to keep this in mind: you are there to serve the people in any way God may show you, and some doors you will have to get through may be very sensitive.

A good example is a man and woman holding hands when out walking. Uganda views this as meaning you are sexual lovers. Kissing in public is also frowned upon. Yet at the same time, two men walking and holding hands is a common sight, and it simply means you are good friends. My co-worker Jesse was raised in San Francisco where the gay community is strong and very public with their affection, like holding hands and kissing between men. When we were headed to do some ministry at a youth prison and walking through the bush to get there, I asked one of our Ugandan helpers to go up and grab Jesse's hand and walk with him. His complexion went from pale to bright red, and he began walking much quicker. Finally, he figured out who put the worker up to it and turned and looked at me with one of those "I'll get even with you" looks, which you do not soon forget. After he was there for awhile, he would grab a brother's hand out of friendship and feel perfectly normal about it.

Whenever you are in doubt about what to do, think, or say about anything, ask someone who's been there for a while to clarify it for you. The more time you take, the quicker you will fit in. God gave us eyes and ears to see and learn with; put them to good use. Do not be one of those know-it-all types who try to bluff their way through, like they know something when they do not. One of the quickest ways to make friends in a third world country is by letting those you meet know just how much you need them. Too many times I have seen missionaries approach those they are serving in an overpowering way, as if the person they were addressing was dumb and they were so much smarter. Granted, often you are going to know much more than those whom you are serving, but the best way to keep a closeness going between them and you is to be humble at all times and keep a servant's attitude.

When you arrive, make sure to spend far more time listening than talking (Ecclesiastes 3:7). When you do talk, do a lot of asking for more answers from your listener and then listen carefully in return. Let him ask you questions about your life and desires and answer back without sounding like you want some big pat on the back when you are finished. God tells us in Philippians 2:1-11 that we should consider others better or higher than ourselves. This is the main ingredient in being a missionary from start to finish—being and staying a servant at all times.

Christ is God, yet He became God-Man as a servant unto all mankind. He left you and me an example to follow in every way without failure. Do not fail to listen more than you talk and you will fit in much faster, have fewer failures, and gain friendships quickly.

Be patient and polite at all times

We as Americans are a very impatient people, as we are so used to the drive up window speed of things on a day-to-day basis. The big problem for us as Americans when entering a third world mission work is that things do not go at a pace we are used to. I have actually seen missionaries who have been there serving for years still calling the local people (or *nationals* as they are actually called) names like "stupid," "dummy," "empty headed," and saying, "You will never learn anything"—the list goes on and on. The only difference between a national's knowledge and ours is that we had education available much earlier in the history of America, and the nationals were hindered by not being allowed to get an education. By saying hindered, I mean they were hindered by those countries that had come and taken over the rule of their country and then, out of fear that the people might get smart enough to gain power back, restricted them from any kind of education. From what I observed, nationals can learn as quickly as we can when education is made available to them. They study harder, use it to gain a new standard of living, and then help others with it when they do get it. Do not look down on other people, but look for ways to bless them in both their spiritual and mental growth.

When you are frustrated, which I was more often than I would ever care to admit, just slow down and take time to think about things. Being patient is not easy for some people, and if you are honest with yourself, you know exactly what I mean. Some visitors who came out thought I was too harsh with some of the people connected with us in one way or the other. Jumping to conclusions quickly is not good either, since it usually ends up with wrong judgment calls being made.

One time, when a couple and their daughter came to our mission, the man went north with me to our clinic deep in the bush. When we arrived, Stephen, our pastor there, told me that the medical staff in the clinic had stolen over two thousand dollars worth of our drugs and were selling it at a little shop down the road. I had brought up a new shipment of drugs and was trying to get it inventoried into stock. The clinic staff was trying to confuse things again so they could possibly steal more drugs. I got very firm with them, made everyone stop, and started the process over with me controlling each step. My harsh voice got their attention, and things were finally done the right way. However, this man did not ask me why I was so harsh with them—he just jumped to the conclusion that I was this way all the time. You can see that there are times when you need to get harsh-sounding, just like you do with your own children. You do this to get their attention and bring about the necessary change, not just to dominate them.

When you are in local offices, you will often be delayed for reasons you do not understand. Sometimes they themselves do not fully understand what needs to be done, or, more than likely, are not paid enough to hurry. Even when you try to buy something and you cannot seem to communicate what you want, do not blow up. Take your time, and if need be go get someone who can translate for you. Remember, you want to make friends with the people, not build a wall between you and them. We had one man working with us who seemed to blow up at people in offices when he thought he was deliberately being delayed. He had to leave the building and drive away in order to cool down. Then, after he was back in control of himself, he went back and apologized. Needless to say, his apology was never enough to make up for the damage he caused for himself in getting anything done the next time. So expect to have hindrances and delays with almost everything you do.

Let people help you, give tips, and say "Thank you"

As I said before, Americans have a bad name as tourists worldwide, mainly due to their superior or better-than-thou attitudes. Make anyone who asks if he can help you feel like you really care and appreciate what he is asking to do for you. Then thank him wholeheartedly with a smile on your face when he is finished. If you would tip for this kind of help in America, then tip them for it there as well. But a little warning here—know your exchange rates so that you do not extravagantly over-tip or else under-tip so badly that you insult the person. The key to making foreign friends is to listen, treat them as equals, and thank them often. You can never thank them enough because they will be giving more of themselves in serving you than you will ever be able to give them in return. At least try with all your heart.

Believe me, they will have you under a magnifying glass from the time you arrive until the day you go home. You must be the same today, tomorrow, and the day after. They will remember all your shortcomings and all the blessings you show them. Honestly asking for their help is one of the best ways you can show them respect, and saying thank you is the best way to gain a lasting friendship and an open ear for the gospel.

One of the best tips or gifts you can give to those who work for you is a personal item, like clothing or jewelry. You can also give them your pocket knife, a pair of your shoes (if they fit), equipment, or extra pay, or simply take them out to eat a nice meal. The nice meal is okay at times, but you must realize that what you pay for a meal out is what they pay for their rent or a month's worth of food. It may make them feel uncomfortable seeing that much money being spent on just one meal.

Sincerely apologize when you blow it

Many times I did things the wrong way out of ignorance, and I needed to apologize to someone. When people see that you really are sorry that you failed to do it right or maybe even hurt them in some way, and you humbly apologize, they will quickly draw closer to you because of it. Most of the poor people in a third world country have leaders who deliberately make them feel like lesser people by putting them down with cutting remarks. Knowing that this is what they get from people in high positions, if you come along and treat them as an equal, you will make them feel very special and appreciated. The more you do this, the more new souls you will win to the Lord, and the ministry will grow abundantly because of it. Better yet, you will grow abundantly as a servant as well, and you'll be able to reach out into new areas with fewer hindrances.

Pitch in without complaining

The best servant is the one who comes out and does whatever it takes to get the work accomplished without complaining. The same goes for where you work in the States—when you have to work around a constant complainer, everyone is miserable. When co-workers are not happy with those they work with because all they do is complain, the listeners sadly end up being complainers as well. Psalm 133:1 says, "How good and pleasant it is for brothers to live in unity." Then in 1 Thessalonians 5:11 we read, "Therefore encourage one another, and build each other up, just as in fact you are doing." Complaining does not encourage, but discourages, and we ought to be encouragers in all we do.

When Christ asked the apostles to join Him, they threw down their nets and followed Him without complaining. We are blessed today because they were obedient and set the example of doing what was set before them. No business or mission can grow successfully when there is too much complaining going on, because too much time has to be spent mending fences. The big problem with any mission base being filled with complainers is that those whom you are trying to reach will see your misery and discontentment and want to turn away. Why should they want to join something they already have plenty of in their lives every day?

When a household is united in spirit and in truth, God will be glorified, and the ministry will blossom into a beautiful bouquet. The whole purpose for being out serving is to win new souls to God's kingdom. We should make sure we eliminate anything that would hinder that from coming to pass. So go wherever you go without a complainer's heart, and be a blessing to everyone you are serving or serving with.

Chapter 27

What are Some Things I can Expect?

Things will take much longer

THE MORE DEVELOPED a country is, the more quickly it can process paperwork. Therefore, the less-developed countries do not have the same modern equipment or the highly-trained people to perform at the same rate of ability or speed. This begins from the time you arrive at the airport and are being processed through all the documentation required to enter, up through all the border crossings, getting driver's licenses, renting a place to stay, getting a mailbox number, obtaining phone or e-mail service, and getting all your utilities. Remember, each place you go will be much slower and less organized than you are used to. Also remember to ask God to help you with your patience since your patience will definitely be tested greatly.

Another major testing will come when you try driving anywhere. Uganda is the third highest in road fatalities, and where you are going may not be much better. Some of this is due to how many cars crowd the main cities where there are very few police to guide and discipline the traffic movement. Please take the time to watch an ant farm and see how one ant gets from point A to point Z. Then take that wisdom with you because these drivers will be just like them. You go through push and shove, no matter where you need to go. If the driver passing you can no longer see your face, he will more than likely just pull over into your lane, since he believes he has the right of way and will take it.

You know how you can react when a waitress is slow about getting your meal to you. Your feet are thumping up and down on the floor, your eyebrows are furrowed so tightly you can hardly see, and your voice is tougher sounding, probably three tones deeper. Now, if that is you at any time when you are home in the States, you might have a really hard time with patience in a third world country. If this is you, please find a way to work on it before you go so you will come back home with some hair left to part.

You will be hassled for bribes ("Chi")

Chi is a way of asking for a bribe without having to actually say the words. Chi is their asking you for money for some tea to enjoy later, but what they really want is some money to take care of your needs. Please be careful never to confront them about their asking you for a bribe. They will become very angry and treat you as if you just insulted them. Just keep your cool, go about what you need to do, and try to act as if you did not hear them. You must do this, no matter how many times they ask you for chi, and keep a smile on your face. Scripture has a perfect passage for you to remember and apply when this happens. Exodus 23:8 says, "Do not accept a bribe (or give), for a bribe blinds the eyes of those who see and twists the words of the righteous." Both ways, you are a part of a bribe, and you are in sin by causing another person to stumble.

The other thing about bribes is that once you start giving in to them, they just keep growing so that there is no end to them. You also make it harder on those who have to follow you past that person. People who take bribes like to brag about who they got to give them their chi. Please make sure you are not the topic of their conversations, sending your Christian witness flowing down the drain. Bottom line: God is always faithful to get you through to the work He has called you to.

You will be stared at often

When you are in America, you are the white page and the foreigner is the black dot in the middle of it. When you are in a foreign country, they are the black page and you are the white dot in the middle of it. You know how you react when you see cult members with the Moonies selling roses near the highway or mall. You cannot help but stare at them and wonder what makes them tick. This is how people in another country may be looking at you. They will wonder just how different you are from them, what you are doing in their country, and how long you might be staying. The reasons may be many—what is important to remember here is that this is a normal reaction to something or somebody they find different. A good reaction is a slight head nod and a pleasant smile on your face. Watch them, and you will see that you have just answered their main question—are you approachable and friendly? The quicker you apply this, the quicker you will make new friendships.

You will not always know what they are saying

This is one of the hardest things to get through when you do not know another person's language. Many times I sounded like I was mentally unstable while I tried to get across what my needs were, when they had no idea what I was saying, nor I what they were saying. Make sure you have someone who knows the language with you to do the interpreting.

Language schools exist in almost anyplace you are called. So find one and at least learn some of the basic greetings and other types of daily-need words to get you by from day to day. When I was serving in Jinja, I gave up trying to learn any one particular language because I had to deal with nineteen different ones almost daily. Having a good interpreter is like finding a rare diamond, and good interpreters are worth their weight in gold. When a person is raised from childbirth with a language, he becomes very fluent in it. When I preached a message on Sunday, I used an interpreter since I knew I could never use their language without stumbling around and thus causing a distraction from the message. I could speak a little in Swahili, but I was quickly put to shame when they started rattling it off faster than I could understand them.

One thing I used a few times seemed to work very well. I went to a village that used a language I was not used to and was greeted in their language. I listened carefully to the greeting and tried to say it back, and I drew some laughter and smiles. But when I got up to preach, I said, "You heard me try to speak your language and I did not do it very well, so I need my interpreter who knows it well so I can bring you God's Word without making mistakes in what God has for you to hear." Then I would say, "I need your help, and you need mine, so I guess we can just be a blessing to each other." Just use some common sense and you will get by; make sure you do not get upset when you cannot get yourself across to anyone.

Here is a little thing I did at times that gave all concerned a good laugh. Many times when I need to buy supplies for one of our building projects, the men I dealt with in English quickly switched to their vernacular language to figure out how much they wanted to jack the price up because they saw me as a white man with big money, at least they thought so.

When they finished their scheming and turned back to me and started talking in English again, I spoke a made-up Oriental language each time they tried to say anything. They kept saying, "I don't understand, I don't understand." I kept this up for a good while, until I figured it was time to let them know that this is how I felt when they switched to vernacular. This gave me a chance to talk to them about cheating people out of money by switching in the middle of the road, instead of being truthful and staying honest all the way through the purchase. I had bought enough supplies over the years there that I was very familiar with most of the prices, and I would only have paid them what I knew it was worth. Yet it was funny to watch their faces when they could not understand the made-up language that we sometimes resorted to and pretended we were speaking to each other. A guy has to have a little fun sometimes. Please just try to work your way through things without getting upset with anyone.

There are weapons everywhere you go

Most of the developing countries are still very unstable, needing to keep a tight rein on the public and other political parties. When you go to the bank, the police or armed guards are there with machine guns; the same is true at the airports or wherever there is much money on hand. Sometimes when we were out walking at night, we saw roving police patrols of maybe six men with machine guns or the like. You quickly learn to be thankful they are out there because there are plenty of gangs running around trying to rob people.

Missionaries or visitors are not allowed to have guns for protection, so we used very tough guard dogs to keep the thugs away at night. At least two to three times a week, the thugs would come to our fence to see if there was a way for them to get in and rob us. Because of our guard dogs, they would back off and leave. We even had to protect our dogs from being killed by poisoned food. We kept them in cages at night, with coffee wire on the cages so the thugs could not throw the poison food in to the dogs. The cages had been made with releases inside the house, lest the thugs think they could just get by because the dogs were caged.

One time, after services at the prison, a group of prisoners were talking to me and said I had some very tough guard dogs. I asked them, "How do you know—have you been to my fence at night before?" The response was worth a million dollars—the stumbling words rolled out of their mouths. I took advantage of the situation and began telling them how terrible our dogs might be. I said they might love to tear off people's faces and bite out their eyes or tear off their skin and rip out their stomachs. The faces they made told me they did not want to find out whether it was true or not.

About two weeks later, as I was buying timber, I was approached by a man who worked in the yard there. He asked me if it was true that my dogs were really that terrible when attacking people, and I said, "They could be getting even more terrible in wanting to chew people's faces off just to hear them scream" (notice the *maybe* or *possible*, so I wasn't lying). Needless to say, our thug visits went way down and fewer beggars came around as well.

When you know ahead of time that there is going to be a show of weapons ahead of you, it is so much easier for you to adjust to. There is nothing for you to over worry about; just use common sense and you should be safe.

Public transport can be very dangerous

I cannot count the number of close calls we had on the road by nearly colliding with someone driving on our side with no lights on or trying to pass on a curve or hill. There are very few policemen compared to the number of people in the country. In addition, when a policeman pulls someone over, he will quickly let them go when the bribe (chi) is placed in his hand. Therefore, you can count on most of the vehicles being in disrepair, with drivers who will demand the right of way from you at all times.

Public transport is the most dangerous thing you will face as a missionary. The drivers seldom own the vehicle they are driving, and they are told how much they must earn for the owner for that day. The driver gets to keep all the money he can make over that amount. So if a taxi has to make three runs back and forth in a day to fill the owner's demand, the driver will drive at excessively high rates of speed to squeeze in at least one or two more runs for his pay. The drivers also overload each trip to make more money per haul, and they end up breaking down often. They do not care about anyone's life coming or going, only about the money they want to make.

Trucks become the worst offenders at night, as most of them are run-down with few to none of their lights working in front or back. Mix that with the bicycles with no warning on them either, and you have a deadly accident in the making.

One night I was headed back home on what I thought was a clear road ahead, when suddenly right in front of me, stopped dead in the middle of the road, was a truck unloading some charcoal, with people standing on my side as well. There was no time for hitting the brakes; there was only time for turning to avoid hitting the people and head for the ditch, which I did willingly. We missed everybody, stayed upright, and made it back up on the road. This happened to me a few other times, and I decided only if there was a serious emergency would I ever drive at night. Danger is always there; just be careful and yell a lot at your taxi driver when he gets to going too fast. He won't slow down, but at least you tried before you died.

The large buses, like our Greyhounds, are mentioned in the paper often when many people are killed because of speeding and head-on collisions. When you can, please get your own transportation, and pray continually for your safety, as it will surely be needed.

Most places you will need to visit are very run-down

This title does not give any idea of how badly things can be run-down or how extremely dirty they can be. Most of the public buildings when we got to Africa were in a war-torn state, with broken windows, bullet holes in the walls, and little to no office equipment left. That has changed somewhat now in the main cities. Not so when you go out to the outlying towns or villages where things can get awfully bad for you.

When you go shopping in an open air market, which is often, you will buy much of your fruit and vegetables from filthy countertops. However, it is when you go for your meat that things tend to get to you somewhat. They hang the whole side of a cow on a hook, and it stays there the whole day. The flies are usually pretty thick by midday. But if you go early, you will end up paying a higher price. Once you have told the man how many kilos you want, he will first chase off the flies, then take his machete and whack off the amount you asked for on a bloody tree stump, then wrap it in a banana leaf for you to take home. Sometimes they have plastic bags called Kavaras.

Most places you will look at to rent will be dirty and in bad repair. The offices you need to visit will be the same way. Just about every place you go is just like this. The other thing you will find hard to do is trust a restaurant to serve you some sort of sanitized food. Just make sure it is cooked well and pray you do not get sick, which we did at times. I think you get the picture; things will be dirty and run-down most of the time.

The amount of filth you will find on toilets is frightening. Carry your own paper, hold your breath, and hope you're quick. Wet wipes would be awesome, and may now be available.

Please do not get too scared off by some of what I have written so far because things are changing and you can be a big part of expediting that change.

What about hospitals, doctors, and medicines?

When we first arrived in 1991 the hospitals were extremely bad. People only went there if they knew they were about to die. No window glass or no screen wire remained. The mosquitoes came in by the truckload. The smell of urine was so strong in every room that you could only stand it for a short while and then you had to run outside for fresh air.

The nurses and the doctors were very poorly trained, underpaid, and corrupt. They would not treat anyone until they were paid a bribe prior to the treatment. The government supplies the hospital's medical needs and pays the doctors, and the patient is only supposed to pay very little. But the doctors steal most of the medicine and then sell it in their own private clinics. The nurses will not pay any attention to anyone who has not given bribe money first. The operating rooms were a shock to me because they were so grimy-looking and very poorly equipped. As I said, most people just went there to die.

Ten years later, things have improved somewhat; most of the wings have been painted and are somewhat clean, and the training of the staff is much better. I am reasonably sure that this is about the same worldwide in regard to third world countries. The bribery is still going strong, and I doubt if it will change any time soon.

Medicines come from all over the world and are as different as night and day in their ability to treat your need. Do some research when you arrive, and find out whom you can trust to sell you only the best types of medicines. Usually there are trustworthy medicines from England or America available at a fairly low price. That is one advantage of being in a third world country; all medicine prices are greatly reduced to fit the annual income of that area. A malaria treatment in the States is around $75, but over there you might only pay $2.

Some missionary hospitals exist and you can find them if you take the time to find out where they are located. They are clean and well staffed but somewhat more expensive. Remember to ask other missionaries who have been there for awhile where these types of things are available. By slowing down and being careful, you can get some reasonable treatment lined up for your needs down the line.

Low housing standards and high rent

Most of the homes you might find that fit your budget are run-down with high rent attached to them. They normally rent out each room to one or more people to live in. So when you have that many people crammed into small areas, things tend to get run-down, very dirty, and highly unsanitary.

When you are from a developed country like America, the landlord looks at you and sees big dollar signs. You have to be patient and work through this type of attitude. One way to do this is to have someone local you know you can trust find what you are looking for and rent it much cheaper than you can. The thing you have to watch out for is your person working up a special split-the-difference-deal with the new landlord behind your back. Remember, the people in a poor nation have had to struggle just to survive most of their lives, and deceiving is part of their everyday lives. Therefore, know your person's honesty before you commit to any long-term rental agreement. Compare rental prices before you commit.

Land can be gotten through the city council office. Most of the time you will not be able to purchase it outright, but you can get it for a forty-five to fifty-year lease agreement, paid annually. They have a listing of properties available for you to see, and you just go check them out. These leases are dirt cheap—in dollars, maybe $75 annually. You just have to prove you will develop it and have a planned program for its use. Again, you can ask those who have been there awhile to get your wisdom ahead of time.

In part one, I talked about the dump of a house we rented when we came to Jinja, where we worked out a rental agreement part of the rent going toward fixing the house and part going toward the rent. We did that again with a much larger house and it worked out as well. Then we received land through the city and built a large complex there.

You will make loving friendships that last

When you first arrive, you see everyone through rose-colored glasses. You do not know their good or bad points, so you just sort of "veg-out" on everything that is happening. You get so excited just meeting people from a different country and having them listen to you. The missionaries whom you may have come to join the work with will be sitting there smiling, wondering how long it will be before your bubble bursts. Now before you think I am not being fair here, wait and hear what else I have to share about these relationships.

Most third world people are raised with little to nothing in the way of luxury in their homes. Food is quite often scarce to nonexistent. Finding money just to stay clothed or go to school is very hard to do. So it's reasonable to say that when you come from a very rich country like America, you are often viewed as if you owned your own bank. Some of your first friendships can be people trying to get money from you by sharing their hardships with you. Now do not get too discouraged or upset at this statement because this will be a common, everyday experience for you to deal with. Most of my lasting friendships started this way, and I worked with them through their weak areas and hung in there until they understood what a real friendship was like.

A good example is when we were busy building housing, churches, and even a clinic. This meant we needed to hire some workers with skills in the areas we needed to get the job done. One carpenter I hired named Grace was the hardest-working, most likeable guy you would ever hope to find.

Then the other side of him showed up, in that he was stealing from the site heavily and very often. The first time was too much to just let slip by, so I ended up having the police go with me to his residence and get back what he stole. When he did it again, I talked the police into letting him work off the debt for what was missing. This happened numerous times, but the amount got smaller each time. I figured we must be making some progress on getting him to eventually stop his bad habit. By the time I left Africa, you could not pay him any amount to steal even a nail from me. His last statement to me was this: "Papa Jay, who are we ever going to find that will love us as much as you love us?"

Needless to say, the longsuffering the Lord does for us works with our problem relationships just as well. This man still calls me long distance on my dime, just so he can hear my voice, and that is worth a million dollars to me, as he is now like a son to me. I found out that I could not out-love any one of the people whom we were blessed to work with. We are a family that will never end, as we will still be able to visit someday in heaven for eternity.

The hardest thing we ever had to do was leaving Uganda for the last time, knowing we might not be able to see the people we had come to love again. We still hope that someday God will bless us with enough funding to travel back just to see one more precious smile and get a long overdue hug. Leaving there was about as close to facing the death of someone, without the person actually dying, as you could get.

As I've said, take many photos. You see, we sometimes get downcast in our spirits because we are thinking of those we left behind and wish we could just walk over and say, "Hi, how are you doing today?" Photos are a big help in this area. We have literally boxes of photos of just about everything we ever did on the mission field.

I hope you understand that, yes, you might have to work through some difficult people and times, but if you persevere with them, your friendships will grow and they will last a lifetime. So go enjoy yourself, and make many new friends.

Never enough hours in a day

Missionaries have one common problem affecting them, and that is there is never enough time to do everything that comes at you daily. There are so many needs and needy people that it is impossible for you to meet them. God tells us in 1 Corinthians 10:13 that He will not give us more than we can bear. This means that when things come at you too fast, slow down and check to see what is really from God and what is not. Remember, you are not the only person God has called to be a missionary, and He will more than likely give a different calling to each person. Just work hard at making sure you are doing what God wants you to do and not just shooting for numbers to write home about. One will be blessed of God; the other is doomed to failure and possibly embarrassment in the end.

A safeguard you can work with will help keep you on the right track. Simply prioritize your work schedule for each week. Then review what has taken place and the outcome of your efforts. When you see that you are not making headway in any particular area, recheck the steps you have taken. When you have researched things properly and given it enough thought and prayer, you can then decide whether you should continue down the same path any longer. It is not shameful to make changes, especially when that issue has really hindered your goals or the work you know should have already been accomplished. Remember, you can always talk to other missionaries in your area and have them pray with you for the wisdom and direction you need to take. Pride has no business in missions, as you will find out quickly if that is a part of your nature. You will not like the embarrassment it will cause you.

You must take time off to rest

Nothing is worse than making mistakes because you are worn out and brain-dead. Trying to recover from those types of mistakes may take a very long time. Some things may never recover at all, like renewing a friendship in which you said something dumb that hindered it. Sometimes you write the wrong word or verse down in one of your messages, and then you cannot find a way out of it no matter how hard you try. Most missionaries work about twelve to fourteen hours a day, seven days a week, month after month. You must be honest with yourself and take time to rest when you're getting too tired. Again, be careful that your pride does not get in the way here, and you think that a co-worker cannot do the job as well as you. Worse yet, you might be afraid that they may do a better job and people will want them to take your place. God called you and God placed you where you are, so trust in His judgment and relax.

The Making of a Missionary

We took trips to the Indian Ocean coastline in Mombasa, Kenya. Sometimes we flew and other times we drove. Either way, we went because we were burned out and needed the rest and relaxation. Believe me, it is not a sin to use donated money to go get much-needed rest. I believe your supporters would rather you spend it on that than on buying a coffin for you to ride home in because your heart just could not take it any longer. Plan to get rest regularly.

Do not be afraid to make friends with other missionaries and go on breaks with them. We had some awesome times with missionaries whose teachings I might not fully agree with, but they are still brothers and sisters in Christ for us to enjoy. Christ took time away from the apostles, and He went off to rest and pray. Therefore, so should you; you will agree with me once you hit the wall and cannot function because you're so tired.

Chapter 28

You Will Face some Dangerous Times

FOREIGN COUNTRIES ARE notorious for the dangers that can rise up when you least expect them. Most of the ministries you get involved with will be as normal as you would hope them to be, so just count them a blessing. Others may have a different chemistry makeup, with danger attached to them most of the time.

We had built a clinic up near rebel territory and I had to go there often. The drive through the bush to get there was long and dirty. I often carried expensive drugs to refill our little pharmacy. I was never attacked, nor did anyone attempt to rob me. But later, the rebels did come and attack that area, and our help had to run on foot for their lives for over thirty-five miles through bushes and swamps. They finally reached safety in a town named Soroti.

I think you can get the picture. God will give you a calling, and that fact makes it His, so you should trust in Him finishing what He starts and not worry about the danger so much. Just stay in prayer, trust in Him always, and then give Him His due glory.

Diseases are always lurking in the shadows

America is very blessed with good preventive medicines and healthy conditions. Almost everything you need is sanitized and modern, with well-trained staff to meet your need. Even then, people still die from illnesses, accidents, or just old age. Therefore, we tend to think that this is status quo everywhere in the world. But in a third world country, the medical support is less than half of what you have in the United States.

Africa is known for having a very high rate of AIDS infection in its population—30-45 percent. Polio and other diseases are there as well and are not well controlled. But the more highly transmittable diseases, such as AIDS, are what we need to be more aware of, and we must know the right precautions to take for our safety. I knew I had the protection of the Lord on my life to accomplish what He had for me to do, but that does not mean I should be foolish and put Him to the test when He has shown me there is a danger lying before me.

We were often called to go and pray for a person dying of AIDS, and we could actually smell that death was near as we entered the room of the sick person. Most of the time he lay on a mat on the floor, his body dwindled away to a skeleton of a frame, and crying with only moments left to live. I would lay down on the mat next to the person, hold him in my arms, and begin praying and crying with him. My hope was to make sure that my Lord and I showed him that we loved him, no matter what had happened in his life.

This usually opened up the dying person's heart to hear the gospel message, and with what little strength he had left, he would accept Christ as Lord and Savior. Often the person died in our arms or shortly after we left. The hardest cases to bear were the innocent little children who had no say in their deaths.

The water in most devastated areas is extremely dangerous to drink unless you boil it and strain it through some fine cloth. When we did a baptism in a river or lake area, we made sure we did it where the water was constantly moving. When water does not move, deadly parasites begin to grow in it. Maybe you can remember what I said before: when in doubt of what to do in any circumstance while on the foreign field, ask those who have been there for a good while what to do, and stay on the safe side. There is always wisdom in an abundance of counselors, that is, if they are wise in the ways of that area. There are other things that can cause you to get diseases, so please ask other missionaries when you arrive about any dangers you may need to know about and what to do to avoid them.

Chapter 29

Expect to see More Miracles

Miracles in America

PERSONALLY, I HAVE only seen a few miracles in my lifetime in America. That does not mean they do not occur; they surely do. What it does mean is that there must be a reason why so few are seen by the public, let alone the church. The main difference I believe is that we only allow ourselves to go as far as "we have the control" of any given situation. When it gets too uncomfortable for us, we exit stage left and head for safer ground, like home. The miracles that you hear about the most in the States usually pertain to someone's illness or accident. Others may be from a host of other issues.

The circumstances surrounding a miracle are often rather common, while others can catch you from the blind side, leave you dumbfounded, and bring you to the earth-shaking reality that God is in control. Never stop believing in miracles, even if you have never experienced one. I can guarantee you this, if you reach out into God's realm, into God's powerful hands, you will see more miracles than you could ever keep count of.

The miracles in a foreign country

Throughout our years of being around seasoned, lifelong missionaries, we have heard so many stories of godly miracles that we could not possibly remember them all. The one thing that was loud and clear was that they all had been in such a set of circumstances that the recipients were totally helpless and there was absolutely nothing else they could do but pray. They hopefully and desperately asked God to bring the answer to their need. As I said before, in the States you can just drive away, call the police, rush to the hospital, have good medical care and medicine available to you, or just use the famous way out of problems—dial 911. Believe me, 911 on the mission field is a fervent prayer being raised up to the Lord, asking Him to handle the problem because you have nowhere else to turn for help but Him.

I have chosen not to include some of the miracles we have gone through over the years here because you can read them in part one of this book.

When you are a missionary, you run into circumstances coming at you so fast that you will not have time to pray over each one of them. God knows what it will take to accomplish what he has set in your path to do, and He will make sure you are able to fulfill it each and every time.

Remember, when things are totally out of your ability to control, God will step in and get it done. If you have any doubt that anything is going to happen from God in the way of a miracle, you may not receive one. However, it will happen often if you just trust and believe He will do it for you in your times of need. He is still in the game of performing miracles; they have not ceased, and they are still going strong. Hope you grab one soon.

Be alert and you will experience them

Most believers are so caught up in the details surrounding an event that they miss God's hand working in and through it. Take time to back off and look deeply into all that takes place, and you will find God in the midst of all you do—be it a miracle or not. Remember, God never leaves us or forsakes us, and that should cause you to realize that nothing is beyond His knowledge or power over what is going on in your life. Read Deuteronomy 31:6 and all of Psalm 18.

Please do not expect God to run down and bail you out of the due penalty of your sinful ways, because He says, "You will reap what you sow" in Galatians 6:7-10. Bottom line is this: God can still perform a miracle in the midst of your sin, if it will bring you to repentance. Yet, at the same time, He might just let you suffer the penalty of your actions so you will not take His grace too lightly. Miracles are always there for the having, but it is God Who makes the decision on how, when, and why they are going to be done, or even seen.

Chapter 30

Having to Work in More than One Ministry

Ministries everywhere are in abundance

PLEASE, THE NEXT time you are at church, take the time to look around during any service and see just how many different ministries are operating to meet the needs of the body. Then save that wisdom, because you will need to remember it when you're out serving. Mission workers do not go out to do just one simple job, because they are called upon daily to take care of a wide variety of needs and ministries.

We had four different prison ministries, a handicapped ministry, an orphans' ministry, a street kids' ministry, numerous village ministries, a medical ministry, a youth ministry, a high yield seed ministry, an in-town ministry, a housing and church building ministry, a slums ministry, a vehicle and equipment repair ministry, and even a school of ministry. Every one of these ministries had many branched-off areas that had to be done in order for them to work smoothly and to grow.

One thing you do not want to have happen is to get so distracted by all that is coming your way to deal with that you do not accomplish what God called you to do or what your leader there have asked you to do. There is always the main goal for you to accomplish and the work you have been assigned to do. Anything else that comes along has to be worked around these two callings. You can prioritize each ministry if you do not set yourself too rigid a line to follow.

One of the things this helps you do is to train the nationals you are there serving. The ministry you are doing must be fruitful, and that includes training yourself out of a job. The apostle Paul was always busy training himself out of a job then checking back on them and making sure they were still steering the path he had set for them to follow.

Chapter 31

How to Prepare for a Furlough Home

Cover your missionary work before leaving

YOU WILL QUICKLY find out how good a job you have been doing when you try to find someone to take your place while you go home on furlough. Too many missionaries who come to serve in a poor nation also think the poor are poorer in mind and/or incapable of learning what you know. This is sad, because anyone given the proper training can, and will learn. We had a friend who ran a somewhat growing ministry which involved teaching pastors, running a day school, and other areas of interest. The thing about him that bothered most of the other missionaries was that he was constantly degrading the nationals. He degraded just about anyone he had to deal with, saying they were too stupid to learn anything. Yet many of his students went on to do some very notable ministries. I guess being stupid means you're smarter than your teacher, because they took what they supposedly could not learn and made something good come out of it. Remember, if all-knowing God can use us, who are we to think highly of ourselves when we are flatly stupid in comparison to Him?

Be a person who encourages those you are training. Then evaluate how well they are grasping the material you are feeding them. Make any necessary changes to make things go better for them and praise their growth often. When you have done this regularly, you will not need to worry about who is capable of taking your place for any given length of time. Remember, just like temptations, God will not give us or the workers we will be counting on more than we or they can bear (1 Corinthians 10:13). Train more than one person at a time to do the work of ministry.

Granted, you more than likely will be working with many who have little to no education, but that does not make them stupid. Most of the time, it is due to having lacked the opportunity of education. This can be due to the lack of money or war or suppression of some dictatorial leadership running their country. The British held the nationals back from education when they ruled Uganda and Kenya for many years. The whole job of a good missionary is to train himself out of a job and then move on to where he can repeat his accomplishments.

Discipline any availability to money just as you would with a young child. You put enough candy in front of a child and he will abuse it. Nationals have not had too many dealings with money issues, at least at the level you probably work with. So do not expect them to manage it as you would. This is not a problem when you are working with other missionaries in the same outreach, but if you are not, try to get another missionary you have made friends with to distribute the money to your help on a set schedule. The main thing is to have the work continue while you are on furlough with as little hindrance as possible. Coming home on furlough will be a pleasure if you have placed people in the right positions and put some trust in them.

Know what you will need to bring back with you after furlough

Many countries you will serve in fall well short of having the goods, materials, or equipment you may need for your mission. Hold meetings early on with the other members of your team to get them to start figuring out what they might need you to bring back for them. What you bring back will more than likely be far cheaper than what it will cost you there, due to import duties on products shipped in. See the section that discusses shipping for more details and the ways to go about getting things there and back.

Most foreign countries will not let you leave there with more than two bags for each person, but you can bring back up to eight per person by going air cargo on your flight for your extra six bags. Just make sure you know your weight limits, as they are extremely strict, and the overage charge will break your bank, not just your back.

Things you might need for your mission work would be training equipment and materials, books, replacement parts for cars or equipment, kitchen goods, building items of all types, new and used clothing, and some good tools, but always called personal as they are yours until you give them away. You do this to avoid having to pay heavy import duties if they are viewed as for possible resale. Please do not forget to bring a decent gift from home as a thank you for the government officials who have helped you get your work going. It's in their culture and they will expect it of you, and it is worth your effort to keep them pleased and on their side for future things. Also, get your national staff some gifts as well. We used to get them inexpensive watches, jewelry, battery-powered games, clothes, and anything else we thought might make them happy. They were always extremely happy, as if we gave them a brand new bicycle, which we have done many times. Believe me, they work hard for you, and will protect you at all cost, so love them in any special way you can think of.

The other thing you need to consider is the team back home who has been taking such good care of the details and support there. Find them nice souvenirs, like good carvings, artifacts, batiks, jewelry, local instruments, and letters and pictures from your national staff. These are just some suggestions for you to consider, but use your own list of ideas and have fun doing it.

Plan well ahead of your departure date

You can get special "See America Passes" that I explained above. You will never be able to travel this cheap inside the United States, so take advantage of it and go see everyone you know would love to see you. But plan it all ahead of time so people can plan along with you and can have the time off to be with you.

Remember that you can lay over in any city along your route going and coming for as many days as you wish. You can plan to see other cities like Paris, London, Frankfurt, Amsterdam, or maybe even Rome. Your budget will need to be considered, but if you plan far enough ahead, you can start saving up for it well in advance while you are doing your ministry.

Another thing to remember is that you might not get another chance to get to see these other countries, so why not take advantage of it while you have the chance?

Sunny and I often had to go through Europe when coming or going, so when we were leaving the mission field we decided to go a different route. We decided to go down through Cape Town, South Africa, which is a very beautiful city, then to Sydney, Australia, which was a blast, then on to Fiji Island for some fun in the sun, then home to America. Because we went that way, we got to see places we would never have a chance to see again, and they are so memorable to us. We stayed a week in each place. So plan ahead and go enjoy. Believe me, you will have earned the time to relax after you have worked seven days a week, seventeen hours a day, week in, and week out. You will be hungering for some down time anywhere. Make sure your support team agrees on your budget for it and that there are no misunderstandings.

Plan whom you will want to see

You know your family and friends better than anyone else. Therefore, you know whom you must see first to keep them happy, and how long you can actually stay for your visit there. Family should always have priority over friends. Remember it is up-reach that is unto God; then in-reach, that is unto your immediate family; then outreach. The direction of your flights might have some bearing on who gets to be seen and when. Your own children must be of the utmost importance on your list of visits, letting everyone else fit in after they are considered.

The next thing you must make sure you do is take the time to enjoy them and yourself. It will cost you nothing to lay over at each stop for a visit. Believe me, when you hit your home church, you will be too busy to get much rest. People will want you to come visit, go out to eat, come over to eat, do guest speaking, go play golf, go shopping, or go to sporting events. However, the going out to eat happens so many times you will think you will burst if you take one more bite. I am not complaining, just stating the facts. Most people will want to show you how pleased they are with what you are doing for God's kingdom. You should let them enjoy their time with you and you with them. You will soon be out of their sight, and you do not want to be out of their minds because your support could suffer.

Make sure you take plenty of photos home. Bring the negatives and, if need be, have more made to give away to people when they ask. We always made sure we took boxes to each speaking engagement and let people pick the ones they liked. This makes a picture connection to what they have been led to support. Never underestimate the value of good photos to give away, as they are priceless. The day will come when you are about to leave to go back to work. You will want people telling you that they will be praying for you, will write you, and hopefully will want to support the work God is doing through you and the team you are working with. So please show them you love them while you have the chance.

Chapter 32

How to Start a New Outreach

Go slowly and check it out thoroughly

MINISTRIES ARE AVAILABLE everywhere you look. The problem is which ones does God really want you to be involved in? When other people are involved in order to take on a calling, they will need to have a say in it, as to whether to take it on or simply pass it on to someone else. God does not run short of servants to meet the needs He wants taken care of. He will manage with or without you and get the job done. So do not think you are the only one capable of meeting everything that comes your way to consider. This is a very important thing to remember about God; He is not a God of confusion, but of organization. Nothing will catch Him by surprise. He never has to say, "Oops, I did not see that coming," or "I do not know why it all went wrong and it failed." God is all-knowing, and that includes everything about you and your abilities. Just make sure you check it out carefully and then wait on the Lord to show you through His Spirit if you should be involved or not. Nothing is worse than jumping before looking and crashing down into the pit called "total embarrassment."

You should know by now that if you do not know enough about something, you need to ask more questions until you actually know. God describes people who tend to be failures in any ministry as fools over and over in the book of Proverbs. Some good verses to refer to about wisdom are Proverbs 3:13; 11:2; 13:10; 23:23; and 29:3. Then, about being a fool, go to Proverbs 10:10, 18:7; 12:15; 12:23; and 14:24. There are many more, but I think you will get the picture. Seek wisdom from those in the know and you will be off to a good start in making wise decisions.

Investigate the needs, the time, and the cost

To start a project or ministry without vital signs to rely on, is like walking in rush hour traffic with a blindfold on. You are headed for certain disaster. Asking basic questions can help in tremendous ways when starting or trying to fulfill a calling. Try using some of the questions below as opening questions in a new venture.

"What might be needed?" types of questions:

1. What is expected of me in this calling?
2. Can I meet those needs with my abilities?
3. Will I need other people involved to do it?
4. What age group or groups are to be reached?
5. What materials will be needed?
6. What permission or licensing needs to be obtained?
7. What government regulations must be followed?
8. Are there more branches of this group I might need to administer to?
9. Will I be ministering to both males and females?

"How much of my time will be needed?" questions:

1. How many times a week or month must I be there?
2. Will I need to be there for an hour or more?
3. How far is it there and back?
4. How much time is needed for discussions afterwards?
5. How much preparation time do I need each week?
6. Will other staff need to give it their time?
7. How long will the ministry need to continue?

"What, if any, cost will be incurred?" questions.

1. What material will I need?
2. Will I need to rent space or purchase space?

3. Will there be a need to feed the people?
4. Will I need benches, desks, or tables and chairs?
5. Will I have to stay overnight and how often?
6. Will I have to pay for extra help?
7. How much are the government fees, if any?
8. Will I need to do any construction to start with?
9. Will I have to pay for utilities?
10. How much will my transport to and from cost?

I am sure you can find many other questions to ask on your own. You can never ask too many questions to start with. Seek answers before starting, every time. Please never fail to do this.

Get good advice

Like I said before about the fool, do not play the know-it-all game and then fail. Seek advice and follow it. Then adjust as you need to.

When I had to build a two-story building on our compound, I had never done much construction work before, so the first thing I did was to evaluate my experience and knowledge. The list was simple; I had previously built a porch, a doghouse, a swing, helped my dad build a little on his house when I was growing up, and done a few other small projects. Therefore, I quickly admitted to myself that I did not have what it would take to build this unless I got a lot of help from some people in the know.

I took my made-up list of questions, went around to those who had the knowledge I needed, and drained them of all they would share with me. I then went back and applied what I had learned. When I hit a wall again, I repeated the process I had started with. This continued throughout the project until it was finished. We ended up building seven churches, a clinic, a four-bedroom house, and the two-story apartments for our helpers. Granted, I still am not much of a builder, but what I gained paid off for the mission, and it is still growing today. I still ask a lot of questions when I do not know something, and I am still growing because of it.

Do not make promises you cannot keep

The tongue can get us missionaries into big trouble, mostly by just being unrealistic about things. When something looks difficult, it more

221

than likely is going to be too hard, too costly, take too long, and the list just runs on and on. Matthew 5:33 tells us that our *yes* needs to be *yes*, and our *no* needs to be *no*. We represent Christ, and when we promise something quickly and do not count the overall cost and then fail to complete it, we damage our witness and the trust of others. Do not get trapped into giving an answer on your emotions. Stop and take time away to think. Listen to this very carefully: go seek God's advice and help and wait until He gives you the answer. Everyone tends to want his needs met immediately. This is largely because the people are suffering and they want their suffering to end.

We cannot blame them, but we will fail them even worse if we promise and then cannot deliver. They get their hopes up, tell everyone what is supposed to happen, and then you come back and say, "Sorry, I cannot do what I said I would do." Hint: notice the "I" used in failures. Being honest about your abilities and seeking God in prayer will make almost all you do become more successful, bringing God His due glory. More of God, and a whole lot less of you, makes for more lasting success.

Take time to smooth out the rough edges

We all have watched track and field events on television, or maybe even have run a race or two in person. The mile long race is one of the best examples I can use. The competitors all line up on the starting line with one hope in mind—getting to the finish line ahead of everyone else. The person who has run in many races over the years will run a totally different race from the one with little experience.

All the racers bend over in a racing stance, feet spread apart, eyes fixed ahead, just waiting for the starter's gun to go off. Then *BANG!* Out of the starting blocks come the runners, striding off toward the finish line. The newest runners tend to get over-excited and accelerate past the other runners and put quite a distance between them. They think, *I'm winning this race because I am running out ahead of everyone else.* The other more mature runners have set themselves a pace they know very well will get them to the finish line. The pace they have learned from experience is neither too fast nor too slow, but it is competitive and up to their ability. The fast starters begin to get into trouble about halfway through the race, their legs begin to fatigue, they start to have shortness of breath, and no matter how hard they try, they keep slowing down, and down, and down.

Now the more experienced racers begin to catch up to them and are still breathing somewhat normally and running at a decent pace. Not much longer, and they race past those who blew all they had in them in just a short distance and a short amount of time. Most of the time, the burst-out-of-the-block runners seldom finish the race, and they end up going home defeated. Do not forget the great knowledge that comes from asking those in the know about what to do. Do not start a project or ministry until you have enough facts to weigh against your abilities.

If you know what you are going to be up against to start with, you can seek out the help you will need to finish what you started. Wisdom always comes from surrounding yourself with others who have more ability and experience. These wonderful people once walked in your shoes, sought out wisdom, applied it, and grew in the process. This is exactly what you will do as well when you follow their footsteps to success. The rough edges all disappear when you take the time to sand them off with gathered knowledge and a lot of hard work.

Train someone there to take your place

Imagine Christ coming and then not training the apostles to continue the work when He left. Should Christ have trained the apostles and then have them fail to train others to carry the message of the good news to other people? We would not have the Word with us today or even be saved were that the case.

I do not think you need to be dragged over the coals on this, but you do need to understand the importance of training others to carry on the work. When serving in a warring country, you are just one assassin's bullet away from total chaos. When you leave like this, you leave behind those whom you were there serving and were supposed to have been training. When you hold the thought that only you can run the show and others will not be capable of doing what you were doing, you leave a big empty void, which means all your efforts will have been in vain. From the first day you arrive until the day you leave, be busy training others to do God's work, not yours. You know deep down in your heart that you want to be found pleasing to your heavenly Father when all your work there is over and others are running the ministry. In addition, God will get more glory when you do it for Him and will reward you in ways that will blow your mind.

The workers Sunny and I trained are doing an awesome job for the ministry and for the Lord. What more could we ask than to know that the work the Lord started through us is growing daily, and a multitude of new souls is being won for the kingdom. Amen to that, my friend!

Chapter 33

Getting an International Driver's License

Getting an international driver's license

THIS IS FAIRLY simple to get. You just need to go to the phone book and find where the nearest AAA office is located. Go there with an up-to-date American driver's license, two American passport photos for each applicant, and ten dollars each. Explain where you are going and that you need an international driver's license to drive while you are there. If I remember correctly, you receive it that day. However, things do change, so ask how long it will take. Always start early in getting these things put in place so you are not worrying yourself to death over last-minute issues.

Getting a local driver's license

This is not a license from the States, but one from where you are going to be serving. Again, you will need two passport photos, copies of your Stateside driver's license, and personal police driving records for the last three years.

Getting a driver's license in a foreign country is not the same as getting one when you are at home in the States. Your vehicle must meet their qualifications and restrictions. Before you even start trying to get a license, find out what they require for your vehicle to pass their testing and inspection. Some will require you to have reflector panels on the rear and a fire extinguisher inside. Sometimes you have to have your mission names painted on the lower door panel and sometimes on the back. You can see by this that you need to do some investigating to find out each of the requirements.

The driver's test can be a bit of a pain in the neck. This begins with an inspection of your vehicle, for which you have to set up an appointment, usually early in the morning, and are seen about noon. Then you will more than likely wait most of the afternoon to actually take the test. They will inspect the vehicle, looking for any failure on your part in meeting their requirements. Should they find that you did not meet them, you will have to go and get it all corrected and then make a new appointment. Be very careful here, as this will also irritate them and they will give you much more trouble when you come back. My suggestion is to search out all the information you can so you will have all your marbles in a row when you go to take your test. When you come back the next time to renew or register another vehicle, they will be much easier on you. They will only do this because you have shown them that you properly respected their time and efforts. This is an important thing to remember: always stay polite, no matter how foolish they may sound, because you will quickly regret the repercussions of not doing so.

The different types of licenses and permits

You will need to be careful here as well. There is a big difference between commercial and personal use. For instance, a van can be used both ways, but not if it is registered for personal use only. This is usually called a PMO, a "Private Motor Operator." You will be assigned the maximum number of passengers you will be allowed to carry. You will have to have "PMO" painted on the front and back of your vehicle, so the police can quickly recognize if you are being compliant with the law. "PSV" on your vehicle means it is a "Public Service Vehicle" and can carry passengers for hire, which you cannot do with a PMO. The same thing applies to a truck and its uses.

As in the States, there are different driver stamps for a car, truck, motorcycle, tractor, or a big semi-truck. Know which ones you are going to need and get them all at the same time. You will need proof of your ability to drive bigger rigs and specialty types of transportation or work equipment. Make sure you have your driver's license for these qualifications from the States with stamps on them or at least have some type of verification of your abilities. If you do not have them, you might not be able to get the license without getting driver's training from a local driving school, which is very expensive. Remember to think ahead and plan things well.

When you are not sure what to do, seek out the answers from those who are there or have been there before. You can do it when you get there, but if you need any documentation from the States, you will find it a bit hard because you will have to use third parties to get them for you. Government offices are notorious for not giving out any kind of information to anyone other than the person on the documents being requested.

Make sure you have someone designated with the power of attorney for you in the states before you leave to go out. You do this for reasons like needed extra passport photo's, taxes at home, or maybe you are killed or die over seas and they need permission for you to be shipped back to the States. You will find many other reasons for having a power of attorney in place, like a death, taxes, banking, and medical needs. So make sure you make this a priority, because if you do not have one, you can be delayed for a very long and frustrating time. Again, I say plan ahead and stay in charge of your needs.

Chapter 34

Health Insurance, Medicine, and Deadly Critters

DENOMINATIONAL CHURCHES HAVE missions departments that set annual budgets for you, covering most of your needs. This is going to be bad news for those who are non-denominational. Buying overseas insurance is way too costly to buy as an individual or for a small family, unless your church has a big budget for their mission program. Most non-denominational churches do not have any type of budget in place to take care of your overseas medical needs. This also includes the lack of any benefits for your retirement years down the line. You will need to budget monthly for both of these needs from your ongoing support. It is important to remember that you cannot be an effective servant if you are run-down or overburdened with worry about getting sick or injured. Budget for it because this is being a good steward of your funding.

Just a reminder—do not go out with a pre-existing medical condition and then expect to lay that cost on your supporters to try to take care of. An overseas missionary has enough problems to deal with without adding their own pre-existing medical problems.

The second part of the difficulty is just trying to find an overseas insurance company that will actually pay off when you enter a claim that needs to be met. It is almost impossible to actually get the company to pay the claim. Do not rely on their assurance of "no problem."

I have talked to many missionaries who had years of experience with this problem, and the same fact just keeps coming up; you cannot get them to actually pay out on a bill. Fraud, lying, fake injuries, and a multitude of other ways I cannot even imagine are filed as claims to these insurance companies' offices daily. They do not trust a claim as being valid and/or without some definite over-billing included. We looked at every possible way to get us personal insurance, but we came up empty-handed, as it cost more than we had funding coming in.

We belonged to a non-denominational church that helped in each of our needs, but it always seemed to cost more than the funds available for us.

Let me clarify. God does not let His children suffer overbearingly, especially those who are out doing what He called them to do. God provides for His children in every way if we will trust in Him without doubting. James 1 clearly tells us how to trust in Him. Yes, you are right; we do suffer at times and that is always a part of our testing and gaining strength as Christians. However, like He did for Job, God puts a limit on it, and then He brings us back up stronger and better off than when we started.

Because of this insurance problem of not wanting to pay out on a claim, the places you would need to use your insurance will not accept it for fear that they will not get paid for services rendered. It sure looks and feels like a no win situation, and it is, most of the time. Just remember to take this time to work out a budget that meets all your needs for today and your tomorrows.

How much to trust locally-purchased medicines

Both good and bad medicines are out there, and you must be careful to make sure what you are getting is of any real value for your medical needs. First start where I told you before—talk to those who have been there for a good while and get a list of places and medical providers you can reasonably trust and believe will meet your needs. We found that most medicines we tried that came from India, Pakistan, Egypt, or a not very well known nation were not all they claimed to be. They gave you a medicine mixed with some sifted powder, and it was being sold for a profit and not for the cure. You can find a good provider if you take your time and check them out well for quality in medical value. Shelf life is dated on the medicine, and the products are available most of the time.

Since I built a clinic, I had access to the government medical stores and got medicines for all the missionaries in our area, as well as for ourselves.

Obtaining the medicines directly guaranteed freshness and quality of all products received. Use your imagination and investigate in depth and you will find answers for just about anything you have a need for. The prices of medicines are much cheaper overseas than in the States. Some medicines are a little higher than others due to import costs and volume of sales. The cost scale would be about ten cents on the dollar compared to America.

Warning: do not start carrying home large amounts of medicines for other people. You will be arrested, fined heavily, and can even go to jail for a long time. The first requirement is that you need an international license for dealing in drugs, have a medical clearance, and have proven knowledge of medical products. Stop and think about it—highly-skilled drug dealers try doing this all the time and are often caught. Guess what? You will be too. You can travel with your own medicines, but make sure you have proof of your need for them if you have a large amount.

Please make sure you know the medicines you are getting are good before you start taking them for any length of time. The repercussions could be deadly or leave you very ill for a long time. Some missionaries even had to return home because of the severe side effects they suffered. Make sure to check it out very well and you will be reasonably safe.

Protection from deadly critters and diseases

Common sense always pays off in the long run, so know what you are up against and take the proper precautions for you and other people's protection. Poisonous spiders, snakes, parasites, and many diseases abound in some other countries. Some snake lethality is measured by how many steps you will be able to take before you drop dead after being bitten.

Spiders are much harder to protect yourself from, especially when you are in strange territory. You can spray for them at home and in your workspace to be on the safe side. A very poisonous spider has bitten me twice. The first time was very frightening as I dealt with the painful effects of the infections that came with it. The second time, I had enough knowledge to react much quicker in getting the right help and medicines. Ignorance is no excuse when the knowledge is available and you haven't taken the time to search it out.

Parasites are also a real danger that can debilitate or kill you. Investigate for possible risk areas when moving about, especially when baptizing or swimming in unfamiliar waters. I know of three missionary young men who died after ignoring the warning given to them not to swim in some very slow-moving water infested with parasites.

Deadly diseases are also prevalent. While some are right out in the open, others are much more hidden, and you had better know where to look for them in order to avoid coming into contact with them. Since Uganda has a very high percentage of its population infected with AIDS, the dangers of it are almost unavoidable. Knowing this, take the necessary precautions to remain safe, but do not distance yourself from people's need for a relationship with Christ.

I never feared holding a dying AIDS victim in my arms and crying with him or her. Some had open wounds that were runny, but I still hugged them and led them into a relationship with Christ. I am still AIDS free, and I believe it was because I was not putting the Lord to the test, but I was meeting the needs He set before me. If God is deeply involved in your being there, He has you well protected. There is nothing special about me, but there is something extremely special about my Lord. God loves an AIDS victim just as much as He loves you and me. He might hate the sin, but He still loves the sinner; if this were not so, we would still be dead in our sins. Amen.

Tuberculosis is still a real danger in third world countries. It can be transferred by touch or coughing. A few of our orphans had tuberculosis, and we managed to take good care of them. They are still with the mission today, and we have not been infected. If proper handling procedures are followed, you will do fine.

What happens if you die overseas?

When you arrive in any foreign country, one of the first things you need to do is register with the US Embassy. You do this so they can know where all the American citizens are and what they are doing while in that country. They are also there to assist you should you be arrested and treated improperly, and to help you find a decent lawyer from their approved list. The listing also includes doctors, good hotels, eating establishments, etc. The thing you hope they never have to do is to help your family or friends send your body home should you die. Some countries are very much against touching a dead body, so the embassy's help is often needed to keep things moving and assure respectful treatment.

You should have a will made before you even go out, no matter what your age is. Do not leave that burden on other people to have to handle, as this is not fair to them at all. You will need to have a list of names in place with your mission team at home and with those with whom you are serving. Make sure you put the names in the order of importance, to maintain respect for family connections. Make sure you have an executor in place to handle everything.

Chapter 35

Retiring from Mission Work

Plan well ahead of time

MISSION WORK NEVER really ends, but the place and time in which you work changes and can have an end. As I have stated before, always train someone to take your place well ahead of time. By well ahead of time, I mean five or six years ahead. The mistake many mature ministry workers make is selling their wisdom, knowledge, and abilities short. What I mean is that you did not learn everything overnight. It took many years of experience to gain your wisdom. I know I found it difficult at times to express how important something was to someone who just recently arrived, compared to a co-servant who had been with me for a few years. A few years of experience can really open a person's understanding to the daily frustrations. Examples include the constant bribery, slow processing, lost paperwork, overcharging, ignorance, and people never being there when they are supposed to be.

You will have taken the time to explain these problems and then given them better ways to handle them. You have also helped them readjust through their successes and failures. Now that they have some experience, they know it is better to listen to wisdom the first time so they will face less interference and frustration later.

No two people who come out to the mission field have the same abilities and desires. You must learn to ask a varied set of investigative questions to learn as much about their weaknesses and strengths as you can. When you have gained more knowledge of what makes them tick, you will also have the knowledge needed to plan your training for them.

Once you have trained people to where you have enough confidence that they will be able to handle running things down the road, you can begin to switch more of your focus toward going home.

We did not know then what we know now concerning what we should have done in preparation for retirement. We should have started many years before our departure date. Some of the questions you should consider regarding retirement are as follows:

1. Where do we really want to settle down?
2. Where is our monthly income going to come from?
3. Will we need to buy a house and furniture, or will we rent?
4. What do we need to ship home, how much are we allowed to ship, and what are the shipping costs?
5. What can we leave behind, and to whom will we give it?
6. Will we still be getting church support, and for how long?
7. Will we need to find a job?
8. Will there be a retirement program available for us?
9. Will we be able to get insurance?
10. Will we be able to be on staff in our home church?
11. How much have things changed since we left?
12. What new laws do we need to know about?
13. What do/can we send to our supporters concerning this?
14. Will the church help with the cost of moving back?
15. Where will we get a vehicle to drive?
16. Do we want to see other countries on the way home?
17. What will our airline tickets cost one-way and for the baggage?
18. Will we need to bring people back some souvenirs?
19. What paperwork is required in order to ship a pet home, and is there any quarantine time?
20. What other questions do we need to ask?

You can see that you need to stop and think things out way ahead of your departure date. A suggestion is to start taking things you want to remember or have a special connection to home on each furlough. If you wait until you are leaving, you will not be able to get them all back, and then you will wish you had taken some items home years earlier.

Another thing to consider about getting things out beforehand is what might happen if the country falls apart security wise. You will have to abandon just about everything there and book it out. Understand that this is a real possibility in any third world country on any given day. One assassin's bullet and things will get out of hand in minutes. I know this is true, as we have talked to missionaries who had to escape from Rwanda during the Hutu and Tutsi ethnic cleansing. They lost everything except what they could throw in their car in about an hour, and then they ran for the border to save their lives.

Complacency is deadly in missions. We found that our leaving things behind was a blessing to the main staff and the nationals we served alongside. We gave them things from America as a departing gift from us. We left clothes, equipment, household goods, vehicles, appliances, pets, over five hundred books in my pastor's library, and anything else we knew we could eventually replace once back in America. They all belonged to the Lord in the first place, and He has plenty more in His storehouse should we have need of more.

So get things in line for leaving way ahead of time and you will leave a bit more relaxed, but you will always be hurting inside to leave those whom you have learned to love so very much.

You will have mixed emotions when leaving

We left under some hard and difficult-to-understand circumstances, so we were hurting in many other ways than what would be a normal departure. One thing is for sure, you will feel like the death of a loved one just took place. Everything inside of you will be hurting. It is not easy to leave the work you were tied to for so many years, day and night, seventeen hours a day, seven days a week, year after beautiful year. During that length of stay, you make many loving friends, and they will become more like family to you than just friends. We raised many orphans who became like our children. To have to leave them behind was an extremely painful event. We cried for months at just the thought of their not being near us where we could give them a big hug to comfort them. Our phone bill was high for many months afterward, due to our telephoning Uganda just to hear their voices for even a moment. I still cry often, even though it has been a few years now since we departed.

Now each day is void of what we were used to doing on our normal day. When your whole life was wrapped up in serving a certain culture and ministry day after day, and now you are no longer doing it, you are a fish out of water. Before retiring, I prepared messages almost daily, and I often did six or more messages a week. Then to come home and sit on the sidelines day after day leaves me feeling like I am of little value anymore to the church. While we were out, others were at home working in the church, filling the positions that we now wish we could have.

Back at home, we wish we could apply all the wisdom and knowledge in us, knowledge that is just bursting to get out and be shared. However, here we sit on the sidelines being onlookers, not participators anymore. I do not plan on being like another dead or dying Christian in the church for long. I can only hope God will allow me to start up a Bible study soon or go around sharing on missions and see what God might want me to do through it for His glory. We will always miss the mission work God allowed us to be a part of for so many years, but we are still open for Him to use us at any time, anywhere, for His glory.

The support drops off very quickly

It is sad to say, but many of the non-denominational churches let their missionaries down by not properly taking care of them after they return home from long-term mission work. There is little to no budget set aside for returning missionaries. The support that was coming in so faithfully while you were out serving quickly disappears when you return home. What is even sadder is that sometimes the church leadership halts the support. When we came home, the church dropped its support funding in just three months. Some individuals keep up their support for about six months. We came home at age sixty-five after spending the previous fourteen years in Uganda, with no retirement fund or visible source of income there for us, with a little savings and no job.

This is what I talked about earlier in planning way ahead of time for your retirement so you will not fear starving to death like we did. I finally got a job doing some security work that barely paid the house payment and some grocery bills. Thank God that my wife was able to work and help out with the bills. Otherwise, we would surely have gone under financially. We had a few friends who checked on us to make sure we had enough to eat, and they kept encouraging us to keep plugging away. Admittedly, we really felt the church abandoned us in our hour of need. But God made sure we made it even without their help.

Returning without an assured income is shocking to anyone who has been used to their funds coming in monthly without ever having to worry about it. People love to take care of God's business and His missions workers, and I thank God for that. However, once you are out of sight, we found out you will soon be out of their minds and budgets too. We can never thank our supporters enough for being so faithful for so many years of dedicated commitment to our needs. May God bless them all abundantly for all they did, and we still deeply love each one of them.

Denominational churches have big missions departments with mission budgets and yearly allowances. There is retirement and housing waiting for you when you return, and even church work is available should you desire to stay involved. That is wonderful as far as funding goes, but I still would rather go out as we did and know beyond a doubt that it was God Who sent us out; it was God Who supported us and not man alone.

I hope in the future all churches will plan ahead for their returning missionaries in all the ways they will need help. God is still in charge and has provided for us when all else seemed to have failed. We choose to do everything we do for His glory, and we will continue to do so until we are home with Him in His glorious kingdom.

What to do with your extra retirement time

This is one area that will differ from one person to the next. I know I have a hard time right now in finding much free time since my job requires me to work some late hours and changes from day to day. What time I do have, I spend it in quality time with my darling wife, Sunny. We go for walks on the beach, or to the dollar movies. Sometimes we go to garage sales or shopping. We do some sightseeing and play games. We do a lot of studying of God's Word and attending church services.

Mostly, we like just sitting, holding hands, and talking to each other about how much we do really love each other and about our children and grandchildren. My talks with Sunny are my most enjoyable times, and I do treasure them highly. She is my life within my life with Christ, and God blesses us daily with more love to share with each other and with others who are hurting and searching for Him. We are now getting more involved in the new church where we have moved on the Corpus Christi coastline. The people in God's house are the same everywhere we go—warm and kind, and we feel loved and accepted. We now had secular jobs that kept us from getting deeply involved, but that is changing now.

We still look forward in hope to going back and visiting the mission work someday, Lord willing. We still make calls there to hear familiar voices, to see how they are doing, and to encourage the work there, in addition to regular e-mails. Who knows—God may want me to start a church here in Corpus Christi; I guess we will have to wait and see, but we are ready in season and out. Amen.

I decided to add the painful story below because it shows how God provided for our retirement funding. Be prepared to be a little shocked by it. Please stay open-minded, and keep us in prayer.

On November 7, 2006, I was riding my Yamaha V-max motorcycle to a men's Bible study at church at about 7:00 P.M. A woman driving a truck made a surprising left-hand turn about fifteen to twenty feet in front of me. I was left with no choice but to quickly lay me and the bike down and slam into her rear tire. I had my helmet on and my leather jacket. Suddenly, I had a mangled body and was lying in the middle of an intersection less than a quarter of a block from church. The driver had just dropped off another man at the Bible study and was headed back home. I'm not sure, but I think she was busy talking on her cell phone, forgot to look in my direction, and decided to just take off.

My left leg was totally crushed from just below the knee to the ankle and was bent back up under my body. My upper body slammed upward into the truck bed, crushing my right shoulder and breaking four ribs on the right side. Then I came slamming back down onto my left rib cage and broke nine more ribs on that side, and one of those ribs ripped open a hole in my lung. My right ankle was cracked, and the back of my left hand was ground almost off, but I was still alive.

Then the lady's truck went on to drive over the rear wheel of my bike, causing my left leg to get dragged a few feet, grinding off a large portion of my lower leg bone. I felt nothing but the loss of my ability to breathe and said a quick prayer to the Lord for comfort for my wife as I thought

I would not make it. Then *bang,* everything came alive and the pain was excruciating.

The next thing I noticed was a bunch of men standing around me; I later learned it was the men from the Bible study who ran quickly to be with me in my moment of need, and they were praying for me fervently. I couldn't make out who was there, but I recognized the voice of my friend Joe and asked him to call my wife to let her know I had been in an accident. I also asked him to be there for her when she arrived. I was so mangled that they would not let her near me when she did arrive. Another brother in the Lord named Walter, who is a doctor, kept me alert and stable until the emergency people got there and loaded me for the trip to the hospital. I stayed awake all the way to the hospital and rode with a pain that I never knew existed. Shortly after I arrived at the hospital, they put me under so I could no longer feel the great pain.

I was under for another two weeks on a bed that kept rotating my body to keep the liquid in my lungs from drowning me. They said I talked to them some, but I have no idea what I might have said to anyone. When I came to, I was still in the trauma ward in level ten pain, and I stayed in that type of pain for another month. They had a tube shoved down my throat and a drain tube coming out of my left side that drained my lungs.

Okay, you get the picture that I almost died from this accident, and I'm now home in a wheelchair, mending bones some eight months later. The thing about this is, first, I could have complained and given everyone a bad time. Or second, I could forgive the one who made a grave error and caused the accident, praise all those who took care of me (especially my dear wife Sunny and the many visitors from the church), and leave a good witness for my Lord. There was no other decision for me to make except the one that would glorify my Lord. A number of the hospital staff started attending church again, and others have a lot to think about—the difference between my choice to be loving and kindhearted or be the big pain in the neck that so many people are while in pain.

The bottom line about this story is that God used the insurance settlement money to pay off our house on the water, guarantee us a livable income until we die, send some money back to the mission to put a few more orphans through advanced schooling of some sort, and provide funds to someday take the cruise we always dreamed of taking. What could have been the end to our abilities to continue paying our bills was instead covered by God's plan for us. All we had to do was stay faithful to Him through all of it, and we did. Amen, and glory be to the God most high Who had our retirement taken care of when man had failed us. I'll admit that it was a painful way to get a retirement plan in place. The payment is long-term suffering and healing. God has brought us through rougher times than this. Our God is an awesome God. Amen.

Please feel free to email us your thoughts and questions, as we would love to hear from you. Our e-mail is (sunnymclaughlin@aol.com).

May the Lord bless you as you bless others while serving Him and them.

In His service, Pastor Jay and Sunny McLaughlin

PW

To order additional copies of this title call:
1-877-421-READ (7323)
or please visit our Web site at
www.pleasantwordbooks.com

If you enjoyed this quality custom-published book,

drop by our Web site for more books and information.

www.winepressgroup.com

"Your partner in custom publishing."

LaVergne, TN USA
24 May 2010

183851LV00002B/16/P